Belief and Understanding

Belief and Understanding

"I believe in order that I may understand."—St. Anselm

Selected Catholic Essays

by Matthew Anger

GLENDALOUGH

Belief and Understanding: Selected Catholic Essays

ISBN: 978-0-6151-9912-2

Published by Glendalough Press
P.O. Box 1001
Richmond, VA 23218
www.glendaloughpress.com

Cover illustration: Cologne Cathedral, 19th century engraving.

Introduction

We live in an age of ugly and reckless polemics. Believers are not only told our God is not great, but that religion "poisons everything"—*everything.* The Catholic Faith especially is mocked and derided. And it is indeed tempting, and perhaps even justified at times, to respond in ferocious kind. But there is another way, a way akin to the path of Catholic intellectuals in the late nineteenth and early twentieth centuries, a method far more irenic, and less polemic, than contemporary friend and foe alike.

This is the way that Matthew Anger shows us, and it is my privilege to introduce this volume of essays, written in the spirit of Salesian charity, a volume that invokes so many of those Catholic intellectuals of that era—Belloc, Dawson, Maritain, Pieper and others. And like these men, Anger is charitable and fair-minded to those at odds with his worldview. But in the end, his irenicism does not lead to compromise.

The Catholic authors of that bygone era sought to illuminate truths for us. Belloc's charming, sometimes fanciful tales, for example, or Dawson's patient, lucid explanations sought to correct misperceptions, not out of spite, but out of charity. And so too Mr. Anger points out that much of what many think is downright mistaken. For example, monotheism is not some social construction of later more "civilized' cultures but is inherent in the earliest cultures. It is polytheism that is decadent. And those who think religious belief is some psychological malady are themselves failing to consider the very real evidence that it is *atheism* that is the product of a distorted, dysfunctional childhood.

His essays remind me especially of an earlier master, the esteemed German Thomist, Joseph Pieper: filled with weighty themes, simply addressed, not confusing the obscure with the profound, the difficult with the true. The Catholic Faith shines in all these essays in its resplendent completeness, put in understandable terms, not overfilled with jargon, not brimming with rancor. These are how essays written in the classical realist style should be: straightforward, yet penetrating as an arrow to the very heart of things.

And it is fitting that one of the best of these essays is Anger's short but solid exposition of Pieper's own wonderful classic, *Leisure: The Basis of Culture.* Anger's essays reflect what leisure is meant to be at its best—not idleness, not childish hobbying—but thoughtful contemplation. Take these essays, then, in true leisure and enjoy and learn.

—Walter M. Hudson

Table of Contents

ᴓ

All Saints and the Sussex Countryside

At about the middle of his life, Hilaire Belloc wrote an unusual novel called *The Four Men.* It is unique in comparison to his other works, and is arguably one of the most beautiful minor classics of modern English prose. On reading *The Four Men*, one immediately feels that it has more in common with a medieval allegory than the popular fiction of Belloc's time. Though the book is currently out of print, the fundamental concepts underlying the novel are worth reviewing. The opening lines, with their Virgilian strain, give one a sense of the whole:

> My country, it has been proved in the life of every man that though his loves are human, and therefore changeable, yet in proportion as he attaches them to things unchangeable, so they mature and broaden.
>
> On this account, Dear Sussex, are those women chiefly dear to men who, as the seasons pass, do but continue to be more and more themselves, attain balance, and abandon or forget vicissitude. And on this account, Sussex, does man love an old house, which was his father's, and on this account does a man come to love with all his heart, that part of earth which nourished his boyhood. For it does not change, or if it changes, it changes very little, and he finds in it the character of enduring things.

On one level, Belloc sought to capture an aspect of southern English rural culture that was fast fading even in his day. On another, deeper level *The Four Men* reveals a

Christianized pagan melancholy and resignation. As the late Thomist philosopher Frederick Wilhelmsen pointed out, Belloc was instinctively drawn to the natural nobility of classical humanism, while realizing that ultimately we must be sustained by faith in revealed truth. Thus unlike contemporary rural sketches, this tale is no quaint and dusty vignette.

The characters are men we all seem to have known, displaying whimsy and melancholy, boisterousness and reflection. They remind us that the common sense championed by the author is not "optional," but truly necessary if our lives are not to be completely intolerable.

Published in 1911, *The Four Men* was based on an excursion that Belloc made in 1902. But he did not complete the book until nine years later. This was unusual for a man who often dictated entire volumes in the space of a week. Originally, he envisioned it as no more than a counterpart to *The Path to Rome*, his nonfiction account of a one-man pilgrimage to the Eternal City. In the intervening years, however, the story was slowly and meticulously transformed.

The plot appears simple enough. The narrator, called "Myself," is joined by three other men—Grizzlebeard, Sailor and Poet. Together they journey on foot across their native Sussex, England, in the early 1900s. Beneath this apparently facile plot is a tale of rich, autumnal prose which appropriately reflects the fading sunlight and falling leaves of late October and early November. It is the time of All Saints. The story thus touches on the fundamental fact of life, which is death.

The nicknames the men agree on amongst themselves. As Myself says, "My name is of importance only to those who need to know it; it might be of importance to my masters had I such, but I have none." Each character might be seen as representations of classic archetypes, or even the

Four Temperaments. They evince unique strengths and weaknesses, yet all serve to complement one another.

Grizzlebeard, whom Myself first meets at a pub at Robertsbridge, is the man of wisdom and experience, or what traditional societies call the "Ancient" of the clan. Grizzlebeard and Myself next make the acquaintance of Sailor. He is the man of the world, energetic, enterprising, restless yet seeking rest. Sailor's dream is to put in his ship at a harbor of final rest. Grizzlebeard, in his somewhat pedantic manner, reminds him there is no such fulfillment this side of the grave.

The band is completed when Poet is met "moving along in a manner quite peculiar to men of a sort… who seem to have no purpose, and yet in some way are by the charity of their fellows kept fed and clothed." He is just what his name implies; the artist with a metaphysical bent and a woolgatherer who seems to lack all common sense. Without the help of his comrades, one wonders how he can even find his own feet.

Reading further, one sees aspects of all three of these fellows reflected in Myself which gives us a key to the real meaning of the characters—they are really aspects of Belloc's own personality. For example, while the sensitive Poet seems the least like the author, his appearance is very curious. Belloc had a high regard for poetry and, above all, desired recognition of his verse rather than his prose works. It may be that the depiction of the Poet reveals a certain embarrassment over the author's reflective and vulnerable poetic side as opposed to the boisterous bardic side. At the same time there is, as with any study of normal and natural men, an element of paradox. This gives rise to the subtle irony by which Grizzlebeard occasionally plays the fool, the

Sailor waxes philosophical and the Poet sometimes appears the most pragmatic of the lot.

Belloc carries off these human portraits successfully because he truly knew himself. As the late Frederick Wilhelmsen explained, he was an "integrated man" as opposed to the "alienated man" of our times who seems not to understand himself at all. Of course, we have taken this alienation to a higher level than the already dysfunctional generations of the past, drowning all thought and genuine self-awareness in incessant noise and distraction. Needless to say that leaves no room for consideration of those things which, nevertheless, continue to haunt us. Our lives become fragmented as we deliberately try to divorce the connected realities of the profane and the sacred. But Belloc, with his feet firmly planted in the soil of Christian culture, could wrestle with the paradox of immortal desires confronting the limits of personal mortality. Wilhelmsen's study (*Hilaire Belloc, No Alienated Man*, 1953) is a favorite of Bellocians, and worth quoting at length:

> The Four Men represent the natural and classical foundation of Belloc's personal integration. He makes his own these archetypes of Western Man of that Western culture in which human nature most fully came into its own. The Poet, the Sailor, and the Man of Wisdom [Grizzlebeard] are the classical unities that underlie traditional Christian values....
>
> Myself is one with himself in these companions. But all the camaraderie, the good fellowship, the hearty wisdom, and the love exchanged between friends is threatened by what one might call the possibility of classical or human alienation. Man is not his own enemy in Belloc's farrago; Death is the enemy. The campfire blazes in the woods and the inn is full of decency and laughter, but the universe in the background breathes mutability and is marked for the harvest.

> The seasons rise and fall. Generation issues into corruption....

> Myself finds his soul in these companions, who part from him after Grizzlebeard warns Myself, Man, to meditate Death. Then "the mist received them and they had disappeared." Myself, troubled in spirit, faces the dilemma Everyman faces. Must this humanity, found and achieved in these four, be swallowed up in the mists? Must alienation, "the saddest thing in the world," claim the soul in the end? Why discover ourselves and then come realize that we have found an illusion? We cannot come to be ourselves finally unless Death itself die in the end. The Night of the Dead has always been the night of their return, and Belloc implies throughout his closing chapter that this prefigures eventual immortality.

Doubt is a natural condition of man. Christ himself expressed the depths of purely human despair from the Cross before commending Himself to His Heavenly Father. Belloc did not surrender to self-centered anomie. Hope transcends the doubt and seeming absurdity of life, just as the story transcends the diversity of the characters and brings out the underlying unity of these four men who at first seem so haphazardly associated.

Belloc, at his best, achieves the utmost artistic economy with a few lines of remarkable imagery. Like other great authors, he can present the known and commonplace as if they were new, and give voice and definition to fundamental experiences. In one scene the four travelers have found an overnight lodging in a forester's hut. Myself says

> I woke the next morning to the noise, the pleasant noise, of water boiling in a kettle. May God bless that noise and grant it to be the most sacred noise in the world. For it is the noise that babies hear at birth and that old men hear as they die in their beds, and it is the noise of households all our long lives long; and throughout the world, wherever men

> have hearths, that purring and that singing, and that humming and that talking to itself of warm companionable water to our great ally, the fire, is home.

A similar passage can be found in Belloc's introduction to *The Old Road*, a study of the ancient pilgrimage route from Winchester to Canterbury. It is an example that deserves quoting as well:

> There are primal things which move us. Fire has the character of a free companion that has traveled with us from the first exile; only to see a fire, whether he need it or no, comforts every man. Again, to hear two voices outside at night after a silence, even in crowded cities, transforms the mind. A Roof also, large and mothering, satisfies us here in the north much more than modern necessity can explain; so we built in the beginning: the only way to carry off our rains and to bear the weight of our winter snows. A Tower far off arrests a man's eye always: it is more than a break in the skyline; it is an enemy's watch or the rallying of a defence to whose aid we are summoned. Nor are these emotions a memory or a reversion only as one crude theory might pretend; we craved these things—the camp, the refuge, the sentinels in the dark, the hearth—before we made them; they are a part of our human manner, and when this civilisation has perished they will reappear.

The four men must separate at the end of their journey, yet Myself confronts alienation with renewed confidence. The cycle of life, which is itself a metaphor that God has given us, tells us that after the Fall and the Winter there is yet another Spring. This makes for a hope that is stronger than mere sentiment or sloppy optimism, and comes across in the whimsical notes which break through the more somber tone. In this respect the book achieves a wonderful balance which is surely a result of that inward "integration."

For Belloc had a delightful sense of the absurd. There is much hilarity, as found in the Dickensian tale of Chief Justice Honeybubble, the retelling of the argument between St. Dunstan and the Devil (with typically Bellocian anachronisms), or the argument over the definition of Cheese. It takes an awareness of reality to make the best jokes. An appreciation of the absurd is only possible when a man already has a grasp of things in their everyday, normal proportions.

One may fairly state that in the realm of fiction, Belloc was less at home than in any other genre, though with his irrepressible energy he managed to produce eighteen novels. Most of these were satires or light-hearted moral tales. Unfortunately the political burlesques have not dated well and only a few of the farces, like *The Green Overcoat*, *The Man Who Made Gold* and *The Hedge and Horse*, remain accessible.

Viewed in relation to these and other books, *The Four Men* represents a transitional stage in the author's life as well as his writing. The earlier *Path to Rome* is referred to as "the story of youth." It is ebullient and even precocious; a realm of bracing mountain air and sunshine in which life's challenges are met with a confident gaze and lusty song. By the time that *The Four Men* was finished Belloc had turned forty and the mood is more pensive. If one has the opportunity to read the book at a relatively young age and re-read it a decade or so later, many of these aspects appear in greater relief. It is a sign of real craftsmanship that the story matures with the reader.

The contrast between *The Four Men* and Belloc's earlier writing was no doubt due, in part, to the disillusionment of a brief parliamentary career (1906-10). Such experiences were a rude awakening to his earlier idealism. Belloc was looking back with mixed emotions upon his rejection of what could have been a promising political career, and, on the other hand the refusal, at the hand of the anti-Catholic dons of Oxford, of a history fellowship, despite his outstanding academic record. Such events threw him out upon the world as an erudite vagabond who had to earn his keep by unstinted output of prose. Yet he was a man of strong convictions who devoted a great part of his life to writing on the most acrimonious topics of the day, even as he confessed to his friend Fr. Vincent McNabb how much it wearied him at times.

Contrary to the notion some people have of Belloc, as no more than a literary pugilist with a chip on his Catholic shoulder, he would have much rather "tended his rightful garden," composing verse and gems of prose like *The Four Men*. It is therefore fitting to close with the lines of the drinking songs that grace his tale, in this instance recounting St. Germanus' victory over the Pelagians

> ...Now the Faith is old and the Devil is bold,
> Exceedingly bold indeed;
> And the masses of doubt that are floating about
> Would smother a mortal creed.
> But we that sit in a sturdy youth,
> And still can drink strong ale,
> Oh—let us put it away to infallible truth,
> Which always shall prevail!
>
> And thank the Lord
> For the temporal sword,
> And howling heretics too;
> And whatever good things
> Our Christendom brings,
> But especially barley brew!

Yesterday's Tomorrow

The quest for utopia is nothing new, but the dizzying technological advances of the modern age undoubtedly whetted our society's appetite for boundless change. Despite the cynicism growing out of the Cold War, the West became obsessed with the promise of futurity which infected all areas of life, including the "Omega Point" of modernist Catholicism as expounded by Teilhard de Chardin. As one commentary states:

> Among the mythologies of happiness, the prospect of a technological Eden, while it was unable to dissipate the more deeply-rooted doubts, nevertheless appeared credible and acceptable. It was an idealized instant, and people thought it might finally be achieved, given that they had conceived it as being accessible within a few generations.... It was to the future that people traveled in order to rediscover that vibrant sense of life than only epic journeys can foster. Among the enthusiasts of the age, a narcissistic concept of destiny became commonplace, and it left its mark in the form of projects for peaceful, trouble-free conquests (Christophe Canto and Odile Faliu, *The History of the Future*, 1993).

At the beginning of the 20th century, such futuristic obsessions were purveyed not only by daydreaming or disenchanted intellectuals, but also by a swarm of pulp novels and magazines that advanced the "idealized instant." Yet this virtual reality in popular entertainment is at least as old as the rise of secular fiction. Nineteenth century novels plotted characters, worlds and worldviews disconnected with traditional culture. The way in which authors like Mary Shelley or George Gissing envisioned life free from the gravitational pull of morality seemed merely to presage later predictions of mankind released from the physical gravitational confines of planet earth. As it turned out, this literary combination of pseudo-ethics and entertainment was to be a constant thread in the genre of science fiction, beginning with H. G. Wells and continuing through the later, more controversial social themes of Theodore Sturgeon, Philip Jose Farmer and Ursula K. Le Guin.

It is interesting to see to what extent this belief in unlimited human potential has succeeded or failed to live up to its expectations and, even further, to what extent such secularist optimism contained within itself the seeds of its own disillusionment. Looked at in cultural terms, the development of futurist writings and films helps us to chart the recurring alternation between optimism to despair. Faith in futurity and materialistic deliverance invariably falls short of its of promises, yet each epoch seems to furnish novel fads to replace old ones, thus fueling new (if transitory) hopes for something better. At all costs, it seems, one must avoid the irksome duties imposed by the created world.

Of the many fairytale predictions translated to the silver screen, one that provides an excellent window on the past century's obsession with progress is Alexander Korda's epic *Things to Come* (1936), based on a screenplay by H. G. Wells. *Things to Come* is remarkably well produced even by today's standards, but the strident futurist vision contains a good deal of unintended irony.

The original movie poster for *Things to Come* boasted of fabulous underground "Glass Cities." Certainly, in a less urbanized past, the vision of a teeming, sprawling megalopolis studded with skyscrapers may have seemed enchanting. In reality, however, the Wellsian landscape has made our society inhuman and appalling. In this vein, it is interesting to note how both socialists and industrialists at the beginning of the century became enchanted with the thought of highly planned communities. According to the Smithsonian's *Yesterday and Tomorrow* exhibit (1994):

> In 1894, an obscure socialist named King Camp Gillette [later inventor of the safety-razor] published a curious utopian tract, *The Human Drift*, in which he outlined his vision of utopia. Gillette prescribed for the future an astonishing collection of 40,000 skyscrapers clustered together in one grand "Metropolis" near Niagara Falls.... [T]he steel-framed buildings would house most of the North American population in cooperative apartments.

H. G. Wells' vision of the future, set forth in *Things to Come*, hinges on a second "great war" in 1940 that lasts twenty-six years, in the course of which Western society is reduced to virtual barbarism. No doubt the scenes of mass aerial bombardment, so soon to become a terrible reality, must have shocked staid London audiences in 1936. After unremitting carnage and destruction, most technology disappears. There are still a few ancient airplanes (air power features prominently in the film) and a derelict Rolls Royce puts in an appearance. It is drawn by two horses in a harness. People are afflicted with a horrible plague and allusions to feudal Europe are conspicuous. After all, the Middle Ages are the great bugbear of the liberal. The city in the film, called "Everytown," is ruled by a local warlord named Rudolph ("The Boss").

While Rudolph is lording it over his backwards serfs, a man named John Cabal puts in his appearance. He has not been seen in Everytown since the beginning of the war and is barely remembered by some of the older inhabitants. Looking remarkably like John Brown in a space suit, he preaches grandly in the third person. Rudolph asks who the stranger is. "*We* are World Communications," answers Cabal. He belongs to the military branch called "Wings Over the World" which represents the "freemasonry of science."

World Communications are bent on annexing Everytown, while Rudolph prefers a more diplomatic solution. The Boss reminds Cabal that he represents an "independent sovereign state," to which the envoy of progress replies, "we do not approve of independent sovereign states." When Rudolph's ragtag army tries to resist, the population is subdued by the "Gas of Peace" which renders its victims unconscious while the soldiers of World Communications parachute into Everytown. Gradually, the gassed population revives... everyone, that is, except Rudolph, who is left conveniently dead.

The film jumps 60 years into the future, 2026, when World Communications have taken control of the globe and Everytown is a teeming underground metropolis of H. G. Wells' dreams. But gleaming cities are not particularly interesting once they are built, and the film attempts to maintain dramatic interest by a conflict between the 21st century progressives, headed by Cabal's grandson (hints of hereditary rule?) and a disgruntled "reactionary" faction led by an artist. The futuristic squabble is over the construction of a new Space Gun which is being used to propel young volunteers into the vast unknown. Some citizens object. However, we are assured that whatever the risks, it is all part of man's unending conquest of the universe.

In sharp contrast with the heroic technocracy established by Wells in *Things to Come* is the nightmarish *Metropolis* created by German director Fritz Lang. Though filmed in 1927,

Metropolis is still considered a cinematic masterpiece. In Lang's production the future mega-city of H. G. Wells is already in place, but the depiction of urban reality is far grimmer. In *Things to Come*, the workers who build the subterranean Everytown are little more than ant-like extras who contentedly operate a vast array of turbines, cranes and other apparatus in a phantasmagoria of synchronicity and big machines. There is no thought for the individual who is completely dwarfed by steel and concrete.

In *Metropolis*, viewers are immediately confronted with scenes of brutalized, exhausted workers who are forced to live with their impoverished families in a gloomy subterranean cavern of drab apartment blocks far below the city of the rich. The proletarians even assume the mechanistic movements of Wells' industrial wonders as they march to and from work, more like zombie automatons than gleeful inhabitants of a Brave New World.

While the leaders of Metropolis spend all their time in business and money making, their children lead a pseudo-paradisiacal existence in their racetracks, pleasure palaces and dance halls. Early in the film, however, Freder (son of the reigning plutocrat) is moved by the spectacle of the workers' plight, and he descends into the surreal depths of the great power plant which fuels the vibrant city to get a closer look. As he does so, one of the over-worked machine operators loses control of his apparatus, causing an over-heated power generator to explode. Amid the noise and smoke Freder suffers a hallucination in which the machine is transformed into a latter-day Moloch, with the workers being driven by their taskmasters into the flaming mouth of the mechanized pagan deity.

Though not essentially Christian, there are a number of interesting motifs in Lang's movie. The legend of the Tower of Babel is interwoven with the story of the founding of the great Metropolis—both the industrial super city and Babel being symbols of man's hubris and greed. On the one hand, we see the degradation of an unfeeling upper class that is completely blind to the despair of its multitudes of human drones. On the other, there is the senseless self-annihilation of the workers driven to revolution and violence by a mad scientist named Rotwang. It is certainly not the vision of modern life that most of us have been raised on.

Americans pride themselves on pragmatism and a healthy disdain for utopian schemes. Yet, if our sense of unreality is superficially different from that of Europeans, it is no less invidious. Our social fantasies have favored the technological paradise rather than egalitarian states dreamt up by Europeans likes Saint-Simon and Karl Marx. One of the first "best-sellers" in this country was the futurist novel, *Looking Backward*, written by Edward Bellamy in 1887.

Looking Backward represented a unique non-Marxian socialist vision of 20th century America, complete with shopping malls, credit cards and radios. Bellamy's generation must have sat enraptured at his predictions of technological marvels and scientific efficiency, but today his vision seems unbelievably bland. Our monotonous landscape of strip malls, car dealerships and convenience stores represents the Bellamyite Valhalla. In retrospect, his vision becomes an unintentional parody of the futurist mind set. It is an interesting commentary on futurism that each set of predictions becomes passé as it is overtaken by the latest advances.

Few readers will remember the great-grandfather of American science fiction, Hugo Gernsback—the mogul of pulp fiction and lurid dime magazines obsessed with fantasy, machinery, entertainment and sex. In 1911 Gernsback wrote the futurist novel *Ralph 124C41+* which set the tone for all that came afterwards. The hero was the deracinated man in a bustling hypertropolis of noise, lights and high rises. Such was the vision promoted quite dourly in the various popular scientific and mechanical journals. As one advocate of urban planning in the 1940s wrote: "Why should our apartments not be as comfortable as certain armaments factories which are soundproofed, dust-free, and provided with air-conditioning and rational lighting?"

If only American men could zoom off to work in jet packs or gyrocopters, or American wives could employ the latest streamlined chrome-plated toasters, ovens and robotic baby-sitters, the world would be a better place. Today we have microwaves, PDAs and plasma screen TVs for the backseat of the car. The hope for material salvation does not give ground readily.

Attempts to radically re-engineer the human condition have failed to solve our social and moral ills. Either man is so perverted that the very devices meant to ensure his advancement become the tools of self-destruction, or else stubborn human nature reasserts itself to frustrate the utopians. Futurism was born of the untrammeled optimism of 19th century industrial progress. Not surprisingly, the mass destruction and pessimism of two World Wars, Communist Revolution and the Great Depression dealt a heavy blow to this sanguinity, giving rise to a new form of literature—the "dystopian" or anti-utopian novel. The most famous works in this category are *We* (1924) by Evgeny Zamiatin, *Brave New World* (1932) by Aldous Huxley, and *Nineteen-Eighty-Four* (1948) by George Orwell. But the best dystopian work of all may be *Love Among the Ruins* (1953) by Catholic novelist Evelyn Waugh.

Waugh's book starts off with a terse sentence which merciless parodies the scientific obsessions of his day. "Despite their promises at the last Election, the politicians had not yet changed the climate." From that point we are introduced to Miles, the main character of the story. Miles lives in an elegant manor, reminiscent of Bellamy's utopian dwellings, in residence with a number of other men. There are carefully manicured gardens, live concerts, stables, and rooms crowded with chandeliers, satin curtains and expensive furniture. Waugh explains that Miles' room "was not one of the grand succession which lay along the garden front. Those were reserved for murderers." It turns out that Miles is a sociopathic arsonist who is undergoing gentle, albeit intensely boring, therapy and mild incarceration to rehabilitate him as a good citizen.

> The State had made him. No clean-living, God-fearing Victorian gentleman, he; no complete man of the renaissance; no gentle knight nor dutiful pagan nor, even, noble savage. All that succession of past worthies had gone its way, content to play a prelude to Miles. He was the Modern Man.

We follow Miles through his unsuccessful romance with a dancer whose failed birth control treatments have resulted in abundant facial hair. Miles indulges in pyrotechnical escapades and suffers additional reprimands by the authorities, all ending in a forced temporary marriage to another woman to ensure his social stability and physical gratification. Unfortunately, his wedding is not destined to last long. He still has his pocket lighter.

To the modern reader, Waugh's story would be hilarious if so many of his predictions had not come true: abortion on demand, ready divorce, and euthanasia. Unlike the majority of liberals, Catholic writers of the period foresaw how the relatively "mild" projections of mainstream progressives would end in holocaust and savagery.

The citizen of the new age lives in a state of constant schizophrenia. On the one hand, he is told that social improvement is right around the corner. On the other, even secularists are making the direst predictions and lambasting their predecessors' failure to improve man's lot. How does one explain this dystopian trend? Catholic poet and critic Roy Campbell saw the crumbling of modernity's optimism over sixty years ago. He said that this "disillusionment depends upon one's having believed that life is in some way honour-bound to progress nicely and pleasantly and finding that it does not do so."

Looking back on the past century of technophile obsessions we see that a popular forecaster like Hugo Gernsback may have been right in the details (he accurately predicted the development of plastic, stainless steel, jukeboxes, television and solar power), but he failed to bring the big picture into focus. Thus, Gernsback does not differ from Karl Marx in proposing a materialist solution for materialist problems. The enemy, of course, is not scientific advancement, but the superstition that makes science and technology a crutch for fallen man. As a false creed it is not new. The Deistic Thomas Jefferson once said in a moment of despair that he could only have "faith in the future"—surely one of the more trite phrases to gain currency in post-Enlightenment society. We can only be grateful that the secular soothsayers are wrong more often than they are right.

G. K. Chesterton's novel, *The Napoleon of Notting Hill* (1904), contains an amusing antidote to futurism's intellectual hubris. He discusses the old game called "Cheat the Prophet."

> The players listen very carefully and respectfully to all that the clever men have to say about what is to happen in the next generation. The players then wait until all the clever

> men are dead, and bury them nicely. They then go and do something else.

Chesterton's ideal of the future is feudal and medieval. While improbable, it represents a future more endearing than that depicted by Gernsback or Bellamy. But more important than the fanciful literary device, *Notthing Hill* represents sanity and the reintroduction of eternal verities. On the other hand, there is the self-deluding progressivist illusion, as summed up by Roy Campbell:

> The dramatization of evolution by its great dogmatists such as Bergson, Shaw and Nietszche has succeeded in inducing a universal state of mind in which all values are immolated on the altar of the supreme deity, Time. To the general mind, therefore, no value exists so much in what actually *is*, as in what is theoretically *about to be*: and even what-it-is-about-to-be is again subservient to what-it-is-in-its-turn-about-to-be. Yet none of these thinkers seem to have stopped to ask themselves why God-in-the-Future should be any more real than God-in-the-Present; or why what-is should be subservient to what-it-is-theoretically-about-to-be, *i.e.* what-is-not.

Chesterton knew that while rampant liberalism has largely stripped man of his noble qualities, human nature remains stubbornly intact, always managing to foil the most absurd schemes in the end. Nevertheless, that same nature can be degraded, and unless we unburden ourselves from the mindset that equates "change" with all that is wonderful, then humanity must endure the new barbarism of idiot savants. The future depicted by Huxley, Orwell and Waugh represents a barbarism brought about not by any impersonal or deterministic force, but by man's own pride which makes him forsake long-term goods for short-term egotistical and material gratification. Men can just as easily, if guided by God's grace, opt for a future that is not perfect, but certainly more congenial to the created order.

Rousseau's Daycare

> But, you know, no one will ever manage even his own household successfully unless he knows all its needs.... But if you can't do anything for one [family], how are you going to succeed with many? – Socrates

The present reputation of Jean-Jacques Rousseau (1712-1778) rests on his formulation of the modern mass state that gave rise to the Republican Terror of the French Revolution. But in his own lifetime, his essays on society, culture, and education had a more immediate impact than his reveries about utopian government. In particular the book *Émile*, published in the same year as the famous *Contrat Social* ("Social Contract," 1762), is considered the founding educational text of the modern age.

Émile was apparently based on Rousseau's brief experience as a tutor for a family in Lyons in 1741—a job which, like many others, he was incapable of holding down for very long. Written as a didactic narrative, this work of pedagogy traces the career of the imaginary student Émile, at the hands of an ideal tutor, from pre-school to young manhood and marriage. The book was widely read and acclaimed, and became the basis of progressive educational theories of Pestalozzi, Froebel and Richter. Its legacy has endured. The sentimental pedagogy of *Émile* laid the foundation for John Dewey, Dr. Benjamin Spock, and others.

Rousseau's educational theories must be seen in light of his overarching social vision. In the same way that Aristotle's *Ethics* was the foundation for his *Politics*, so *Émile* is meant to nurture the ideal citizen of the *Contrat Social*. According to political scientist George H. Sabine, Rousseau's polity departed from older rationalist conceptions. Previous writers identified "morality with rational self-interest [which] at least presumes freedom of private judgment." But Rousseau's "ethics of sentiment" need not do so, "especially if it stresses sentiments that are equally native to all men."[1] This meant the exclusion of prudence from the list of virtues and the belief that social (or group) morality is more important than that of the individual.

Not all of Rousseau's contemporaries were impressed by the lax thinking that was cropping up in both theoretical and popular literature of the day. Sir John Hawkins, in his Life of Samuel Johnson (1787), offered some relevant observations while criticizing the novels of Lawrence Sterne:

> [Sterne] too was a sentimentalist, and wrote sentimental journeys and sentimental letters in abundance.... Of the writers of this class or sect it may be observed, that being in general men of loose principles, bad economists, living without foresight, it is their endeavour to commute for their failings by professions of greater love to mankind, more tender affections and finer feelings than they will allow men of more regular lives, whom they deem formalists, to possess. Their generous notions supercede all obligation: they are a law to themselves, and having good hearts and abounding in the milk of human kindness, are above those considerations that bind men to that rule of conduct which is founded in a sense of duty. Of this new school of morality, Fielding, Rousseau and Sterne are the principal teachers,

[1] George H. Sabine, *A History of Political Theory* (New York: Henry Holt and Co., 1945), p. 579.

> and great is the mischief they have done by their documents.[2]

The prophet Jeremias proclaimed that God "returnest the iniquity of the fathers into the bosom of their children after them" (Jer. 32:18). Error seems to have a cumulative effect, if left unchecked. Rousseau's mother died at his birth and his father, a dissipated and violent man, paid little attention to his son's upbringing and finally deserted him. The absence of parental affection leaves a pathetic mark on all his writing. "Does not the child need a mother's care as much as her milk? Other women, or even other animals, may give him the milk she denies him, but there is no substitute for a mother's love." (*Émile*, Bk. I). Rousseau was a dysfunctional child let loose on a society that was losing its own moorings, with a declining faith in God and sagging moral stability. In this respect he was very much a child of his age.

Just as important as familial and societal antecedents was Rousseau's intellectual genealogy. The empirical thinking of the early eighteenth century claimed to take in the whole of human life. It was believed that a divinized human rationality was a sufficient guide to personal conduct if properly developed. Unfortunately for the devotees of reason, their desiccated creed tended to ignore or denigrate the emotional side of man, as if embarrassed by those forces which refused to submit to man's "pure intellect." By contrast, the Romanticism of Rousseau acknowledged (and indeed, exaggerated) the irrational element in human life. Unfortunately, it was not an improvement. While the Romanticists took for

---

[2] Sir John Hawkins, *The Life of Samuel Johnson, LL.D.*, ed. by Bertram H. Davis (New York: Macmillan, 1961), p.97.

granted their forefathers' prejudices, they inherited little of their patience or discipline.

Rousseau accepted Hobbes' concept of alienated individuals who made up the "social contract," yet rejected the early rationalists' pessimistic view of human depravity. Instead, the sage of Geneva favored the new trend in optimistic and messianic political beliefs that were taking root in France. The ideal state of the Contrat Social would be achieved through revolution, which envisioned not Hobbes's equilibrium or consensus of competing wants, but rather a collective state with an altruistic dedication to a *Volunté generale* ("General Will"). Only in such a state, Rousseau asserted, could the natural man exist and be truly free. As for the family, Rousseau acknowledged it as the most ancient and natural of all societies; but sought a short-cut around it, stating that the association of parents and children is a purely conventional arrangement and needed only so long as its younger members cannot provide for themselves.

At the heart of any intellectual heresy lies a religious vision. In contrast to the practical atheism of Voltaire, Rousseau's vision embraced an impassioned Deism that was to become the fashion under Robespierre and St. Just with their feasts to the "Supreme Being" built on the altar of thousands of dead "tyrants" (and other ordinary citizens). Rousseau's vision of natural religion forms the most celebrated chapter of *Émile* in which the imaginary Vicar of Savoy—a sort of proto-modernist cleric—explains to his pupil a lofty creed which has no need of dogmas and accepts Christ's excellence, if not His divinity. While the author held a vague belief in the afterlife, the dream of building "God's Kingdom" on earth came first.

Rousseau was in accord with later radicals, like Baron d'Holbac, in believing that human ignorance was not insurmountable. Man was not the inherently flawed creature that the Church made him out to be; a creature who, while capable of doing good, was nevertheless inclined by his fallen nature to pride and evil. "God makes all things good; man meddles with them and they become evil," pleads Rousseau. "[T]he first impulses of nature are always right; there is no original sin in the human heart." Accordingly, the "entrance of every vice" can be traced to the repression of man's noble instincts by tyrannical institutions (*Émile*, Bk. I). Of course, Rousseau never explains how institutions, made by men, lead to corruption if all men are inherently good.

In his work on education, Rousseau presaged Nietschze's idea that the enlightened man is really "beyond good and evil":

> The very words obey and command will be excluded from his vocabulary, still more those of duty and obligation; but the words strength, necessity, weakness, and constraint must have a large place in it.... It is no part of a child's business to know right and wrong.... (*Émile*, Bk. II).

As Rousseau says of his imaginary pupil:

> When you leave free scope to a child's heedlessness, you must put anything he could spoil out of his way, and leave nothing fragile or costly within his reach. Let the room be furnished with plain and solid furniture; no mirrors, china, or useless ornaments. My pupil Émile, who is brought up in the country, shall have a room just like a peasant's (*Émile*, Bk. II).

The psychology behind Rousseau's pedagogy is that sin is primarily, or even exclusively, a matter of bad environment rather than bad choices. He might have said, ban expensive jewelry if you don't want people to steal. It reverses the Christian ethic that it is not things which corrupt us, but our use of such things. Rousseau unconsciously acknowledges his own lack of self-discipline in seeking escape in a system which does not "oppress," yet which removes all "evils" by abolishing responsibility. Its counterpart is the daycare state that wants to legislate worldly ills out of existence. Needless to say, Rousseau's combination of total "freedom" and total "equality" is contradictory and unattainable, and the best explanation of his theory is that it is absurd.[3] But that has not kept others from embracing a philosophy that appears to excuse their own irresponsibility on humanitarian grounds.

Rousseau's success no doubt lay in the fact that many of his observations about pedagogy, if platitudinous and rather prosaic, were occasionally tempered by commonsense. He was, for instance, correct about the importance of the mother's role in the education of children. Yet thinkers operating from Deistic philosophies are bound to posit the norms of behavior in things too far below, or too far above, man as he really is, as understood by classical natural law theory.

The constrained vision of Adam Smith, by which the individual "pursuing his own interest... frequently promotes that of the society more effectually than when he really intends to promote it," was in certain respects a reiteration of individual initiative and responsibility found in Aristotle and Aquinas. In contrast to the busybody distractions of Rousseau and d'Holbac, Smith's emphasis was on fulfilling personal duties with a view to the actions of Providence. But

---

[3] J. L. Talmon says: "It was of vital importance to Rousseau to save the ideal of liberty, while insisting on discipline," believing that true liberation came through submission to the General Will (*The Origins of Totalitarian Democracy* [New York: W. W. Norton & Co. Inc., 1970] p. 40). Thomas Molnar explains that all utopian thinkers believe in the paradox of "unrestrained human freedom" and "at the same time, they want so thoroughly to organize freedom that they turn it into slavery" *(Utopia: The Perennial Heresy* [New York: Sheed and Ward, 1967], p.8).

Smith and his peers were cut off from the traditional body of Western thought by the fissure that had developed in intellectual life since the Reformation. In that respect, modern thinkers have tended to represent a welter of reactions and counter-reactions to each other rather than genuine philosophical solutions to existing problems. The institutionalized envy of radical egalitarianism was partly in response to the institutionalized selfishness of pure individualism, as when Rousseau complained that existing laws are "always more concerned about property than about people, since their object is not virtue but peace" (*Émile*, Bk. I). There is a certain amount of truth in this, especially when applied to the pragmatic consensus-based polity of the Hobbesian-Lockean tradition.

As one moves away from philosophical truth enlightened by Christian revelation, the acquired truths and morals of civilization gradually deteriorate. Fr. A. D. Sertillanges states that, "Each truth is a fragment which does not stand alone but reveals connections on every side. Truth in itself is one, and the Truth is God."[4] To seek either liberty or equality without reference to true authority must lead to social fragmentation.

Unfortunately, in the wake of the French Revolution some conservative writers made the mistake of viewing the problem primarily as a quarrel between equality and liberty. In other words, while Rousseau and other advocates of *etatisme* represent one extreme, proponents of extreme liberty occupy the other end of the spectrum. Rousseau's own philosophical confusion shows that such a dichotomy can be

---

[4] A.D. Sertillanges, O.P., *The Intellectual Life* (Westminster, Maryland: The Newman Press, 1959), p. 30.

misleading and is itself a consequence of the breakdown of classical realism.

> Liberalism does not vary [says Robert H. Bork]; it is always the twin thrusts of liberty and equality, and these never change. What distinguishes apparently different stages of liberalism—classical liberalism from modern liberalism, for example—is not any difference in liberalisms but a difference in the admixture of other elements that modify or oppose it. Liberalism itself (putting aside, for the moment, its egalitarian element) is nothing but an effort to struggle free of restraints on the individual.[5]

Liberté, Egalité, Fraternité became the slogans of the French Revolution. Divested of their traditional meaning, these concepts simply turned on and cannibalized one another.

> The great thing is to be kind to our neighbors. Among strangers the Spartan was selfish, grasping, and unjust, but unselfishness, justice, and harmony ruled his home life. Distrust those cosmopolitans who search out remote duties in their books and neglect those that lie nearest. Such philosophers will love the Tartars to avoid loving their neighbor (*Émile*, Bk. I).

Rousseau was a writer who abounded in unintended irony. His comments on brotherly love may well have been a swipe at Voltaire who was the inventor of modern philanthropy—the creed of loving one's neighbor from a distance. Yet Rousseau was no better, espousing improved ways of rearing children even as he abandoned his own. Like the man who "loves the Tartars," the sage from Geneva found it easier to treat of the "general rather than the particular, and consider… man in the abstract" without definite moral

---

[5] Robert H. Bork, *Slouching Towards Gomorrah* (New York: Regan Books, 1996), pp. 57-58.

and social responsibilities, however mundane and unexciting.

It is also true that Rousseau "never loved men more warmly than when he seemed to be drawing away and fleeing from them."[6] This strange combination of altruism and arrogance, egalitarianism and libertarianism, is typical of later dreamers, like H.G. Wells, who envisioned mass regimentation for humanity, but would brook no control over their personal morals.

"At all times and in all societies," says political scholar Crane Brinton, "some men feel that they have abilities which are denied free-play by existing social, political, and economic restrictions." In particular, the frustrations experienced amongst a certain class of aimless educated men "is likely to be rapidly reflected in the alienation... of the intellectuals."[7] Brinton cites as an example of this the failed literary ventures of Brissot and the unsuccessful scientific studies of Marat prior to 1789. These men were suddenly delivered from a life of self-inflicted mediocrity by the storming of the Bastille and the cult of the "New Man." No longer need one strive for socially acceptable qualifications when ideological qualifications would suffice. Thus Brissot and Marat were quick to join the ranks of the "professional revolutionaries" whose careers were fed by the impetuosity of Romanticism, engendering a fundamentally adolescent view of the universe. Not surprisingly, Rousseau was an invaluable role model of emotional and ethical caprice.

Herein lies the sin at the heart of the exaltation of sentiment. The Sage of Geneva declaimed against the "effeminacy" of sensuality, yet preferred the company of

---

[6] Ernst Cassirer, *Rousseau, Kant and Goethe* (New York: Harper & Row, 1963), p. 11.

[7] Crane Brinton, *The Anatomy of Revolution* (New York: Vintage Books, 1965), p. 62.

women to men. It was not that this passionate champion of equality believed in equality between the sexes. Quite the opposite. Yet never having outgrown his earliest weaknesses, he sought out women as props for emotional and physical comfort. Not surprisingly, his noble expressions of matrimonial felicity and child-rearing were belied by the abandonment of his five illegitimate children to foundling homes as soon as each was born. Neither was he capable of pursuing regular employment. The champion of ideal society could only lament:

> I was never made for society where everything is compulsion and burdensome obligation.... As soon as I can act freely I am good and do only what is good; but as soon as I feel the yoke of men I become rebellious and headstrong—and then I am nothing (*Rêveries*, VI).

Beneath the lofty excuses, Rousseau was a moral escape artist. This failure forms a common thread in the lives of many revolutionary thinkers. We are reminded of Karl Marx whose vast tomes of materialistic dialectic, reduced to their primary essence, derived from a personal aversion to work and a negligence of family responsibility that was a scandal in his own day. Marx believed that Communism would provide the "completely unrestricted development and exercise of [man's] physical and mental abilities." He imagined a world when men could choose what kind of work to perform, when to work, or perhaps not to work at all.

Apparently the frustration of the spoiled child who cannot assert himself in society resulted in the "alienation" which is at the heart of Marx's theory and which concept was inherited from Rousseau. This primal abandonment of responsibility, however, cannot be concealed by the pedagogical fantasies of Rousseau any more than "modern parenting" advocacy can hide the dereliction of those adults who needlessly consign their children to institutionalized guardianship under the socialistic state. It is undoubtedly a fear of personal responsibility, goaded by the doctrine of modern secularism that has helped build the modern day-care regime that caters to grown-ups as well as their unfortunate offspring.

As for the Sage of Geneva, he died even as he lived. Sympathetic writers acknowledge that in later life Rousseau displayed a pronounced arrogance which repelled erstwhile admirers. This, in turn, fostered a growing misanthropy. After wandering about and importuning friends and acquaintances, as he had done for most of his adult life, the itinerant philosopher returned to Paris in 1770—from which he had been banished for his seditious tracts—and completed his celebrated and egotistical *Confessions*. Rousseau's dread of secret enemies grew out of control and he retired to the countryside at Ermenonville, where he died suddenly in 1778, at age 66. His life and death thus appear as an embodiment of Socrates' warning: "For so many are in such a hurry to pry into other people's business that they never turn aside to examine themselves."

The Man Behind the Mask

In Oscar Wilde's popular theatrical farce, *The Importance of Being Earnest*, John (a.k.a. Ernest) Worthing declares that "it is very painful for me to be forced to speak the truth. It is the first time in my life that I have ever been reduced to such a painful position, and I am really quite inexperienced in doing anything of the kind." Flippant witticisms like this presented Wilde exactly as he wanted to be seen by others—a brilliant champion of paradox and the *bon mot.* Yet one may wonder if, as in Cecily's reproach of the suavely complacent Algernon, there is not a double entendre: "I hope you have not been leading a double life, pretending to be wicked and really good all the time. That would be hypocrisy."

According to Catholic biographer Joseph Pearce, in *The Unmasking of Oscar Wilde* (Ignatius Press, 2004), the famous poet and playwright more than once made use of artistic dissimulation to achieve candor about his own "double life." He was, says Pearce, a man of many masks through which he alternately concealed *and* revealed his real self to others. Ironically, it was through his artistic mask that Wilde most often spoke the truth, while his personal mask, the one that most people encountered, projected a false sense of sophisticated bravado that sheltered an insecure soul.

Every man is to some degree shaped by his pedigree, and Wilde was no exception. Born in Dublin in 1854, to parents who were members of the old Anglo-Protestant aristocracy, the young Oscar was an early victim of his father's bigotry and his mother's eccentricity. Lady Wilde had a congenital habit of shocking others and casually collecting rebellious causes as they suited her inclination, be it Schopenhauer's philosophy or Irish nationalism. She even flirted briefly with Catholicism. According to Pearce's account, when both Oscar and his brother Willie were under five years of age their mother had them secretly baptized by Father Lawrence Fox while staying at a farmhouse outside Dublin. But Sir William was quick to express his intense aversion to the "Scarlet Woman" of Rome even as he pursued extramarital relations and sired children out of wedlock.

Sexual irresponsibility (on the part of both parents, as it turns out) was passed on to young Oscar and must have found little to combat it in the increasingly relaxed atmosphere of British Protestantism and the elite "public schools," which emphasized manners more than morals. But there were other, purely intellectual dangers for a young mind in the making.

"It is awfully hard work doing nothing," says Algernon in *The Importance of Being Earnest.* "However, I don't mind hard work where there is no definite object of any kind." As Pearce makes clear, Wilde's academic aptitude belied his moping, languid appearance. The young man handily took away prizes at Trinity College for poetry and Greek. Nor was he deficient in physical prowess, as Oscar's peers discovered when they made the mistake of underestimating the strength of this ungainly but robust Irishman. Unfortunately, these early and relatively effortless conquests had their downside. They engendered capriciousness and lack of self-discipline.

Oscar's time at Oxford (1874-78) was especially formative, and encouraged a flamboyant dandyism that was apt to make enemies as well as friends. Most importantly, says Pearce, these qualities made him a living legend at the school.

> [His] adopted character became an adept caricature.... The chrysalis of conformity would crystallize itself into a singular nonconformity with Wilde emerging from the process as a rare and outwardly beautiful butterfly, a dandy dilettante in disguise. Henceforth Wilde's disguise would be a statement, and his statements a disguise. The truth and the mask would be one. Wilde, as the world would know him, was born.

Yet Wilde's undergraduate days were not entirely given over to frivolities. Despite his father's best efforts the young man dived into the religious controversies of the time and made the acquaintance of zealous Catholics at Oxford—a development that was frowned upon not only by Sir William, but by teachers and tutors as well. At times Wilde was more Catholic than the Catholics. "By the beginning of 1876, Wilde was making no secret of his Catholic sympathies," notes Pearce, even at the risk of boring acquaintances who had no interest in such matters. Wilde was surprisingly receptive to the logical presentation of the faith as found in Newman's erudite *Apologia* and *The Grammar of Assent*, and drolly remarked that it was "very strange that [Protestants] should be so anxious to believe the Blessed Virgin conceived in sin."

Despite such outspokenness, some of Wilde's friends realized that this early flirtation with "popery" was more an infatuation than true love. A short while later he would enter the Masonic Lodge. Yet Wilde's attraction was not so much insincere as immature. In subsequent years it developed into a kind of love-hate relationship, no doubt because as much as he tried to shake it, the redemptive message of Catholicism continued to haunt him. While it is true that no man can be "reasoned" into the faith, early exposure to the apologetic works of Newman effectively discredited the spiritual and historical claims of Protestantism, clearing the field of serious religious rivals. All that remained was a decisive moral crisis—the turning point in any man's conversion, including Oscar Wilde's.

After leaving Oxford, Wilde discovered other distractions. By the early 1880's he, along with artist James McNeill Whistler, became one of the fair haired boys of the aesthetic movement.

> For several years before his arrival in London, the [aesthetic] creed had been promulgated, in different shades, by those who had been formative influences on Wilde's intellectual and artistic development. The more ethereal aspects of the movement were represented by Rosetti and Pater, its sensuality by Swinburne and its pseudo-Catholic medievalism by Ruskin.

Following on the scholarly amorality of the English aesthetes, Wilde made the acquaintance of Joris Karl Huysmans' infamous novel *A Rebours* ("Against the Grain"), which represented the logical depths of Pater's more restrained debauchery. In this book, which Arthur Symons called "the breviary of decadence," Huysmans proclaimed a new creed—a kind of hedonist existentialism which maintained that truth was merely the quest for the new and the fascinating. Thus for the superior aesthete, the experience, or the carefully cultivated mood, was an end in itself.

Illustrative of this belief was a letter Wilde wrote to a friend in 1886: "To be master of these moods is exquisite, to be mastered by them more exquisite still. Sometimes I think that the artistic life is a long and lovely suicide...." And again he said, "I myself would sacrifice everything for a new experience" (adding cynically, "I know there is no such thing as a new experience at all"). Yet the licentiousness of Wilde's public banter and artistic criticism seems difficult to reconcile with his more edifying works of poetry and prose. Pearce provides a clue to this incongruity. Discussing the writer's mature period, it is clear that *The Canterville Ghost* and *The Happy Prince and Other Tales*, "abound with Christian imagery and mysticism" in which faith is rediscovered. "However much Wilde may have been struggling with his own faith, it always emerges triumphant in the stories. It is almost as though he is using art to escape from the wretchedness of his life."

"As ever Wilde's contradictions pose a conundrum," Pearce continues. "Were they result of muddle-headed inconsistency or evidence of deliberate evasiveness, a desire to remain intellectually incognito?" Pearce suggests that—with the exception of *The Importance of Being Earnest*—the contradictions voiced by his characters "are uttered for effect, intended to entertain. Contradictoriness was not Wilde's orthodoxy, it was his pose."

Wilde' supernatural tale, *The Picture of Dorian Gray*, is in many ways the epitome of the author's ambiguity. Modern reviewers like to parrot his truism that "There is no such thing as a moral or an immoral book. Books are well written, or badly written. That is all." Yet the novel quickly undermines the author's stated thesis. Prominently featured in the story is a "yellow book" that Dorian receives from Lord Henry, which exerts a palpably evil influence on the main character. The volume in question, as Wilde later confirmed, was Huysman's *A Rebours*.

As Wilde's contemporaries were well aware, *Dorian Gray* drew heavily on the author's own life. Unfortunately, when it was published in 1890, critics tended to concentrate on the more notorious autobiographical touches, acquainted as they were with Wilde's shameless exhibitionism and libertine views. Yet in between those lurid passages which evoke the sybaritic and narcotic atmosphere of the decadent lifestyle are some revealing glimpses of Wilde's inner spiritual turmoil:

> It was rumored of [Dorian] once that he was about to join the Roman Catholic communion; and certainly the Roman ritual had always a great attraction for him. The daily sacrifice, more awful really than all the sacrifices of the antique world, stirred him as much by its superb rejection of the evidence of the senses as by the primitive simplicity of its elements and the eternal pathos of the human tragedy that it sought to symbolize.

Like Dorian, it was often rumored that the author was "on the verge of becoming a papist." Creative writing apparently freed Wilde from deeply ingrained inhibitions. He could express indirectly the attraction that the faith held for him in a life-long battle between the sordid and the sacred that ended in his reception into the Church by Fr. Cuthbert Dunne as he lay dying in a Parisian garret in 1900.

Intentionally ignoring the moral of his own tale, Wilde seemed bent on obeying the malignant advice of Lord Henry, who told Dorian to "cure the soul by means of the senses." Wilde threw himself into deeper and more unfulfilling acts of self-indulgence, ending in an abyss of homosexual promiscuity that Pearce details unflinchingly albeit with discernment. It is as if his profligacy was not so much an end in itself, as the writer pretended, as it was a means of distracting him from the relentless nemesis of conscience. Pearce also confronts what he views as the pharisaical ethical standards of nineteenth century England. Much of his criticism is justified, though one is reminded of Chesterton's objection that "Victorian morality" became a sort of straw man to later critics, and that the society of that time was hardly the first to put hypocrisy into practice.

In one sense, as Rochefoucauld said, hypocrisy is the homage that vice renders to virtue. And it is clear that Victorian society had not completely repudiated the moral standards of Christianity, though it made the mistake of denying their dependence on revelation and supernatural life. A sort of safety-net was still intact, if badly frayed. It was not unlike those restraining moral forces at work in earlier times when ever-present vice was countered by a strong Catholic presence:

> Thus, at that epoch [seventeenth century France]... and even in those dissipated souls at the height of their license, belief existed; whatever may have been the surface of the waves or the swelling of the storm, below was faith: souls returned in time, and the great souls rose high... (Sainte-Beuve, *Portrait of Abbé de Rancé*).

Though far from the strong faith of earlier times, there were limits even to Victorian decadence as seen in Wilde's trial and imprisonment for "gross indecency" (a euphemism for sodomy) in May 1895. One may opine about the double standards and unfairness of Wilde's peers, and the fact that the man who was responsible for the trial, the Marquess of Queensbury (the father of Wilde's lover, Alfred Douglas) was hardly a paragon of virtue. He was an irascible anti-Christian who alienated both his wife and son. Yet Wilde's conduct had been notorious and his seduction of young men and frequenting of male brothels was a scandal to all, even many fellow decadents. Perhaps worst of all was the effect this was having on his devoted wife Constance. His egotistical irresponsibility in that regard tended to alienate erstwhile friends like John Gray and André Raffalovich—both of whom later converted.

The judge's sentence of two years hard labor was severe, perhaps (given the unreformed prison system of the times) unduly so. Yet it was a chastisement which momentarily halted Wilde's downward spiral. Pearce appropriately treats the years at Reading Gaol as his "purgatory." Wilde's imprisonment was a living fulfillment of Boethius' paradoxical assertion that the worst punishment for a soul in this life is *not* to be punished for his misdeeds. Nearly broken at first by the unfamiliar austerities of penal servitude, Wilde later confessed to a friend that suffering was not so much a mystery as a revelation: "I was happy in prison.... I was happy there because I found my soul." Captivity offered a new kind of freedom that loosed him from the bonds of temptation that had vexed him for years. His ensuing journey to Christ, though still fraught with difficulties, was reflected in Wilde's repentant missive *De Profundis*, which he wrote before his release from prison in 1897.

Reading through Wilde's ordeal one is reminded of a spiritually penetrating passage of *Dorian Gray*. The protagonist undergoes a false conversion, congratulating himself on having momentarily refrained from evil after a spate of infamous deeds: "A new life! That was what he wanted. That was what he was waiting for. Surely he had begun it already. He had spared one innocent thing, at any rate. He would never again tempt innocence. He would be good." What Dorian seeks is reform without repentance. It is a false escape that fails him in the end. Likewise having sought for so long to evade his moral responsibilities in the most extreme manner it is not surprising that Wilde's final road to conversion was not the gradual progress of the pilgrim but the halting and arduous ascent of the penitent.

Most of the biographical spadework on Wilde has already been done, though *The Unmasking of Oscar Wilde* includes some valuable pieces of correspondence hitherto overlooked. Even more important than research in a book like this is its interpretation. By contrast, Pearce says of Richard Ellmann's recent treatment of Wilde, "it is fairly comprehensive in facts while it remains largely uncomprehending of truth." Indeed, it is worth remarking just how little effort Pearce has to exert to reveal the Catholic dimensions of Wilde's work. Only crass bias can explain the misrepresentation of most modern studies.

Over the years the deathbed conversion story of Victorian England's foremost wit and debauchee has made its way as a short entry into journal articles and literary surveys. But until now, no one has offered a comprehensive Catholic account of this difficult genius. *The Unmasking of Oscar Wilde* finally fills that void. Nor is it merely a "religious monograph," since it covers all aspects of Wilde's life and personality. The treatment is rich in anecdote and detail without ever losing itself in a wilderness of mere trivia, being held together by a clearly stated analysis of the poet's lifelong struggle between the image that he projected of himself and the real soul beneath. Pearce fully conveys Wilde's artistic accomplishments, and the intellectual milieu in which he moved, while his troubled relationships with friends and family are poignantly told. By the end of this remarkable book, the reader will have followed Wilde on his journey from the sordid halfway house of vice to the humbler but more joyous home of faith that he had always sought but hesitated to enter.

Maritain and the Writer's Responsibility

In his novel, *The Disciple* (1889), French Catholic writer Paul Bourget tells the story of philosopher Adrien Sixte, who lives a quiet, unassuming life in Paris. Yet the professor's works—advocating materialism and positivism—wield a terrible influence over an admiring but unstable student whose actions, in turn, lead to the tragic death of a young woman.

The point of Bourget's book, frankly admitted, is that every writer is accountable for what he writes. "No man of letters, however insignificant he may be," he says in the preface, "but should tremble at the responsibility.... May you find here a proof that the friend who writes these lines has the merit, if he possesses no other, of believing profoundly in the seriousness of his art." Few authors make the moral analysis of their writings as easy as Bourget. Fortunately, in his ethical tract, *The Responsibility of the Artist* (1960), Jacques Maritain approaches the issue with same sensitivity as the novelist.

The neo-Thomist philosopher says that the main source of confusion about art and morality is that they function in seemingly autonomous realms. There is a level in which art, like the work of any skilled craftsman or technician, operates independently of ethical considerations. "A man may be a great artist and be bad man." The failure to acknowledge this fact can lead to errors on the part of the agnostic and the moralist alike. But this differentiation does not imply a complete disconnect. Man is composed of body and soul. In this life the two are distinct, yet inseparable. Maritain explains that

> From the point of view of Art, the artist is responsible only to his work. From the point of view of Morality, to assume that "it doesn't not matter what one writes" is permissible only to the insane; the artist is responsible to the good of human life, in himself and in his fellow men.

Maritain believes that "because an artist is a man before being an artist, the autonomous world of morality is simply superior to (and more inclusive than) the autonomous world of art." In response to agnostics who insist on creative autarchy, Maritain says this is a fallacy born of "a confusion between Art taken in itself and separately, which exists only in our mind, and Art as it really exists, that is, as a virtue of man.... The motto *Art for Art's sake* simply disregards the world of morality, and the values and rights of human life."

The famous French novelist (and contemporary of Maritain) Georges Bernanos often complained of "preachy" writers. Yet he was equally offended by authors who claimed to be Catholic even though their writings betrayed sin and despair. He was critical of the controversial works of Francois Mauriac. For him, Mauriac was "the tortured author of so many books in which despair of the flesh sweats on every page, like muddy water from the walls of a cellar." Maritain voiced similar complaints.

The point here is not to offer a critique of Mauriac's prose, which went through many stages of literary and moral development, but to acknowledge the legitimate concerns about Catholic fiction which cannot be obviated by claims of fame or talent. Nor have these concerns diminished since the time of Bernanos and Maritain. We see increasing concessions, not only by avowed liberals, but even on the part of more conservative writers, who have taken graphic depictions of sex and violence as the norm. This illogical divorce between faith and ethics results in cultural antinomianism and a split personality on the part of many Christians.

Some champions of the modern fictional format explain that novels cannot be heavy-handed, "faith-promoting" tracts, but must be alive and necessarily ambiguous and multifaceted. But here we run up against other, potentially dangerous ambiguities, that have plagued Catholics (writers and readers alike) in the last few decades. Truth expressed indirectly within the analogous form of the novel can be more powerful than a direct statement. For that very reason any concern raised over morality in fiction is a testament to the potential of the novelist's craft which surpasses that of many other mediums for its universality and accessibility.

The moral laxist may sidestep the matter and claim that portraying vice in lurid terms does not necessarily glamorize it. Oscar Wilde had a less naïve view of man's concupiscence:

> The public has an insatiable curiosity to know everything, except what is worth knowing. Journalism, conscious of this, and having tradesman-like habits, supplies their demands.

Wilde was theologically sound on this point. Obscenity and undue curiosity are in fact directly related. As St. Thomas explains in the *Summa Theologica*, inquisitiveness becomes a vice "when a man desires to know the truth about creatures, without referring his knowledge to its due end, namely, the knowledge of God." He cites St. Augustine's admonition that "in studying creatures, we must not be moved by empty and perishable curiosity; but we should ever mount towards immortal and abiding things."

The televised "reality show" is an apt example of what the theologians warned about.

The incautious writer tends to forget that vice is appealing because our fallen state inclines us to irrationally choose lesser goods over greater ones. The restraints of reason diminish as we focus on the immediate acts of vice, in themselves attractive, while our awareness of the long-term consequences of those acts fade into the background. That is why people often engage in self-destructive behavior, like drug abuse or alcoholism, while fully cognizant of the dangers involved. The idea that we can depend upon *pure and unspoiled reason*, free from the gravitational effects of Original Sin, is a well-known point of view endorsed by many writers—but it is not Christian.

At the same time, concern expressed about the explicit and desensitizing qualities of contemporary works of fiction is not a denigration of those mature themes which are often an inseparable part of good creative writing. Catholic novelists should not feel restricted to the sort of unsophisticated fiction penned decades ago by Canon Sheehan or Msgr. Owen Francis Dudley. Indeed, authors like Evelyn Waugh or Flannery O'Connor were able to push the envelope as far as they could without breaking it. But the point at which we make the transition from factual discussions of adultery to details of lascivious activities, puts us in the realm of voyeurism. The recent obsession with—and philosophical justification of—shameless curiosity reveals a dysfunction that is far worse than the old time burlesque or risqué comedy.

The main challenge about morality in the arts is one of definition. But for Flannery O'Connor the measure was intuitive: "Obscenity is obscenity." Sadly, since her time there has been tremendous equivocation on this point. Rather than let the Church set the moral criterion, many practicing Catholics have followed the world's standard which is, quite simply, to have no standard at all.

As O'Connor explains, the Catholic artist can only address delicate topics when his approach is both religiously and morally mature. "Do not make the absurd attempt," she says, "to sever in yourself the artist and the Christian. They are one, if you really *are* a Christian." It is this very fixity on metaphysical grounds that allows one greater freedom aesthetically without being hampered by false, worldly standards.

> Christian dogma is about the only thing left in the world that surely guards and respects mystery. The fiction writer is an observer, first, last, and always, but he cannot be an adequate observer unless he is free from uncertainty about what he sees. Those who have no absolute values cannot let the relative remain relative; they are always raising it to the level of the absolute.

O'Connor added:

> The Catholic fiction writer is entirely free to observe. He feels no call to take on the duties of God to create a new universe. He feels perfectly free to look at the one we already have and to show exactly what he sees. He feels no need to apologize for the ways of God to man or to avoid looking at the ways of man to God. For him, to "tidy up reality" is certainly to succumb to the sin of pride. Open and free observation is founded on our ultimate faith that the universe is meaningful, as the Church teaches.

Readers may recall that Feodor Dostoyevsky takes the same frank approach in his novel *The Brothers Karamozov.* But in his case, as in the stories of O'Connor, this candor operates neither randomly nor gratuitously. It concerns itself with realism about moral and physical deformity, not graphic vulgarity. In a *New York Times* interview in 1955,

O'Connor dealt with the matter bluntly. The error of obscenity, even in art, is that "it draws attention to itself and away from the plan of the work." By contrast, an example of what she would call "a reasonable use of the unreasonable" is her brilliant short story, "The Partridge Festival." Few works of literature have more candidly conveyed the unglamorous nature of depravity without actually resorting to it.

To what extent a modern author can speak to his readers colloquially without "dumbing-down" his morals is something that deserves further treatment. It may be that the trend towards verisimilitude, or "realism," of the last century was justified. But the aesthetic approach of a writer like Flannery O'Connor lies in the realm of opinion not ethics. As Maritain put it, "There are no precepts in natural law or in the Decalogue dealing with painting and poetry, prescribing a particular style or forbidding another." This distinction between aesthetic and moral quality explains why it is possible for the Catholic to appreciate the artistic merit of non-Christian writers who still respect the reader's intelligence.

Given the widespread decline of moral expectations in our society, criticism of contemporary fiction must be reasonably stated. Yet the mere acknowledgement of this decline obliges us to be candid as well. While few authors are guilty of overt nihilism, there is a temptation for the Christian to dilute his art for the sake of marketability. In such a case, producing "popular" and "profitable" novels will completely neutralize a writer's God-centered perspective. The danger of casual artistry on the part of a self-professed Catholic is that it sows greater confusion than openly decadent mainstream literature, which makes no claim to Christian inspiration. It gives readers a false sense of security, as if there are "sin free" methods of vicariously engaging in immoral behavior.

The last refuge for ethical evasion is cultural relativism. "These things are out there and we can't just ignore them." To fill one's books with obscenity is thus a matter of supposed honesty. But therein lies the utilitarian implication that morality itself is a sort of pious falsehood. Maritain was uncompromising on this point:

> It is also possible, and probable, that the moral conscience of an artist whose work is really pernicious is contaminated by questionable human inclinations, warped instincts, or resentments or vices, which he shelters behind his art: then he will claim… that his work is innocent and incapable of offending morality, and is even the greatest tribute ever paid to virtue. But this is not a solution, it is a fake, or an escape.

The Church is not blind to subjective situations and the changes in society's customs and expectations. It will always shape its responses in accord with the dictates of prudence and charity. But the objective standards remain unchanged. As Christopher Dawson said, "The recovery of moral control and the return of spiritual order have now become the indispensable conditions of human survival."

Inventing Hitler

The CBS miniseries, *Hitler: The Rise of Evil* (broadcast May 18 and 20, 2003), directed by Christian Duguay, represented the most lavish film on the Nazi leader to date.[1] It offered fascinating glimpses of Hitler's youth and rise to power, hitherto unexplored in a major movie. Extensive recreations of the Western Front in the First World War, the Beerhall Putsch in Munich and the closing shots of the massive funeral for President Hindenburg after Hitler's accession to power are fine examples of the cinematic possibilities of historical recreation. But while the producers explore many facets of the Nazi leader, they end up formulating new stereotypes without substantially correcting old ones.

Given the historical and physical resources at Duguay's disposal, and the undeniably good elements of the movie, one wonders what went wrong this time. The CBS series shows some of the people around Hitler in a realistic light. This is true of Ernst Hanfstaengel and his wife—the wealthy couple who financed the Nazi movement in the early days. Not even Goering, Goebbels and Hess, playing mere bit parts, are the menacing brutes one would expect them to be. Their unbelievable mildness seems to be a foil to the incubus-like Hitler (played by Robert Carlyle).

---

[1] This review was written prior to Oliver Hirschbiegel's impressive film *Der Untergang* (The Downfall), released in 2004, which is a corrective to Duguay's movie, and accurately details the last days of the Nazi leader in the Berlin Bunker.

> Americans generally prefer to regard [Nazism] as a wild and wicked aberration—one man's or, if his purposes were widely shared, a whole crazed people's. But their nagging fascination with it marks their failure to push it safely beyond the political and human pale. They fail not least because Hitler was about as sane as the next fellow. So were the Germans who followed along as he led them where he said he would. Theirs was a moral madness at worst.... For Nazi power politics and political ethnicism and ideologized mass violence differ only in degree from everyday twentieth-century public life the world over" (Rudolph Binion, *Hitler Among the Germans*, 1984).

It is unfortunate that for all the mobsters and mass-murderers Hollywood has portrayed on screen, it has never managed to get beyond the stock-in-trade Fuehrer as madman routine. By comparison, some years ago Robert Duvall played Joseph Stalin in a creditable HBO production. Duvall captures all the vicious bullying of Communism's Great Leader by means of carefully-studied physical and verbal mannerisms that do not deteriorate into over-acting. Carlyle's performance is simply a more psychologically vehement rendering of the Hollywood dictator. He takes a few of Hitler's intemperate traits and works them up into a painfully monotonous display of on-screen neurosis. The Fuehrer of this film would have landed in a lunatic asylum, not the Reichstag.

Admittedly, Duguay's movie conveys the adulation that Hitler received from the crowds that increasingly flocked to his Wagnerian oratory. But it fails to communicate the charisma that elicited this adulation. Carlyle's Hitler seems not so much Mephistophelian as apoplectic. By contrast, one German staff officer explained that

> Hitler had a magnetic, and indeed hypnotic personality. This had a very marked effect on people who went to see him with the intention of putting forward their views on any

> matter. They would begin to argue their point, but would gradually find themselves succumbing to his personality, and in the end would often agree to the opposite of what they intended (Gen. Hasso von Manteuffel, quoted in *The German Generals Talk* by B.H. Liddell-Hart, 1948).

Much of Hitler's behavior was a product of his milieu and was even expected from an agitational politician. That the man *did* irrational things is not surprising. He was extremely arrogant and often petulant. But this is not clinical insanity. His shouting and raving could be calculated, as when he browbeat President Hacha into submitting to the German occupation of the Czech state in 1939. The Nazi leader indulged in his trademark harangue only to joke later among his followers about the way he had terrified the hapless Czech leader.

Despite his posing and bombast, Hitler was a fastidious bourgeois Austrian in his tastes and temperament. He craved gossip and pastries in equally large amounts. In small groups he liked to indulge his penchant for mimicry and biting humor. Perhaps the closest any English-speaking actor has come to presenting a "human" Hitler is Sir Alec Guinness in *Hitler: The Last Ten Days*. While shown as increasingly incoherent and suffering from Parkinson's Disease, even the aging Fuehrer betrays signs of superficial charm and banality which form a curious contrast to his tirades. The recent film *Max*, by Dutch director Menno Meyjes—about Hitler as a young artist taken under the wing of a Jewish art dealer, Max Rothman—also deals with its subject in a more complex manner. But far more typical is *The Bunker*, in which Anthony Hopkins, as a psychopathic Fuehrer, seems to be rehearsing for his Hannibal Lecter role.

In 1936, Hitler proclaimed:

> That is the miracle of our times: that you found me—that you found me among so many millions! And that I found you is Germany's fortune.

Such hubris is astounding. Yet it appears to have been the one constant in his life, even in the days when he was chronically unemployed, dejected and afraid that the great movements of history had passed him by. Hitler might be called a visionary in search of a cause, though he was ultimately his own "cause" in search of a vehicle. The consistent theme in his life, as revealed in oratorical utterances and passages of *Mein Kampf*, is that both people and ideas are seen through the lens of power.

By all accounts, Hitler's youth consisted of large doses of indolence and daydreaming. He never held a steady job and was forever drawing up plans for rebuilding cities and changing society. These patterns would continue until 1945, when the Fuehrer would brood over architectural models for the "renovation" of Linz, Austria, while hiding in the Berlin bunker. Fundamentally self-absorbed, his character was marked by extreme contrasts.

Before World War I, he shirked the duty of peacetime military service. Yet in 1914, he enthusiastically signed up for a Bavarian regiment when war seemed to offer a release from the tedium of daily life. And when, just four years later, Germany collapsed into defeatism and socialist revolt, Hitler was undoubtedly more distraught at the effect that it had on his own life than on the nation. He lapsed into despair only to be metamorphosed by his first taste of active political life.

Hitler had already developed a fascination with the power of mass politics after seeing protest marches by socialist workers in pre-war Vienna. German historian Joachim Fest reiterates the inchoate urges that dominated Hitler's life before the Nazi party. "[W]e will be tempted to ask whether politics ever meant more to him than the means he employed to practice it: rhetorical overpowering of his enemies, for example; the histrionics of processions, parades, and Party Days; the spectacle of military force applied in war." In other words, behind any political career lies a pre-political impulse.

According to historical philosopher Eric Voegelin, there is a concupiscent force underlying all secularist ideologies—the *libido dominandi* (will to power). Everything else is an afterthought or a series of theoretical justifications. As to what makes these narcissistic social schemes so contagious is that they provide a similar "justification" for the ambitions of millions of others. In that sense Hitler tapped into the grievances and profane aspirations of his time, just as Rousseau or Marx did theirs.

It is a motif played out in every generation, differing only in its fads and trappings, not in its underlying psychology. Hitler would perhaps have been another nameless dissenter had it not been that at a specific point in history his anxieties and insecurities were shared by millions of others who believed, or wanted to believe, that he could offer temporal redemption. According to Hitler's own admission, it was the seething masses of discontented Germans who shaped him as much as he shaped them. For once, his judgment was accurate.

Another failing of films on Nazism is their inability to explain the factors surrounding Hitler's rise to power. Opposed to Hitler in *The Rise of Evil* are the Communists, who remain an anonymous lot, and the German journalist, Fritz Gerlich (played by Matthew Modine). The CBS series, however, provides scant background on the anti-Nazi writer who was eventually killed at Dachau. Two years before his arrest, Gerlich received an anonymous letter. It denounced

Christ "who was born of a Jewish whore" and proclaimed the "birth of a new Aryan religion" which would free it from the "Jewish, Christian, Marxist plague." The specifically anti-Christian invective gives us a better idea of who Gerlich was and why the Nazis hated him. According to historian Ian Kershaw

> Hitler's brutality, contempt for human rights, warmongering, and elevation of force to a principle of political behavior, were all castigated in Catholic publications of the early 1930s. One Catholic weekly above all, *Der Gerade Weg*, published in Munich under the editorship of Dr. Fritz Gerlich—murdered in Dachau in 1934—and Fr. Ingbert Naab, kept up a relentless assault on Hitler, describing him in September 1932... as 'the incarnation of evil' (*The 'Hilter Myth'*, 1987).

But there is no acknowledgement of Gerlich's Catholicism in the film. It would seem that if Hitler was no more than a lunatic, then Gerlich was no more than a TV reporter transported seventy years back in time.

At the same time, *The Rise of Evil* manages to convey some of the animosity that genuine conservatives felt towards Hitler's movement. Not surprisingly, however, it fails to explain why people feared Marxism, and the role of the radical left in Germany's downward spiral into extremism after World War I. Communists in the film appear as flag waving protestors who are kicked around by pugilistic brownshirts. The reality is rather different. Following the defeat of the Hohenzollern and Habsburg monarchies in 1918, leftist revolutionaries made their bid for power, hoping to copy Bolshevik success in Russia. In Hungary, for example, Bela Kun initiated a short-lived but brutal commune that killed off hundreds of opponents. Similar episodes occurred in Berlin and Munich. These "proletarian" uprisings were resisted by a frightened populace.

Among the anti-Communists were freebooters and adventurers like Ernst Roehm, who would eventually become the cadre of the Nazi party. But at that early stage, ordinary citizens and discharged officers also took up arms against the Communists. The difference is that they just as quickly put down their arms and tried to resume their ordinary lives while the extreme nationalist *lumpenproletariat* remained dangerously active and disgruntled. They were not interested in a return to normalcy. They opposed international socialism with national socialism and sought a political messiah who would champion their cause.

Yet at this stage Nazism's crimes lay largely in the future. Hitler could understandably capitalize on the fears of Bolshevism in light of the thousands executed and the millions starving and suffering under Lenin's regime. Unfortunately, the CBS miniseries was too busy reading history backward. If the producers had bothered to look at recent studies by Richard Pipes or Anne Applebaum, they would know that the Soviet system established the precedents for Nazism not only ideologically but pathologically. As Hitler put it, he would "oppose all terrorism on the part of the Marxists with tenfold greater terrorism."

Speaking of Hitler, Stalin once said that if "he didn't exist we would have to invent him." Many, besides the Soviets, have benefited from this outlook. Hitlerism conveniently becomes a form of collective madness, perpetrated by monstrous fiends (not individuals like ourselves). Evil is kept sufficiently remote. At the same time this definition of "evil as Nazism" ensures that all other moral failings must pale by comparison.

Director Menno Meyjes, replying to those who fear a realistic portrait of the Nazi leader, said: "If you say Hitler is a monster and always was a monster, you remove the element of choice." Because wickedness is no longer understood as a fundamental moral problem—which involves personal decision and accountability—we can only see our villains as being unsavory in every detail. (In Duguay's film Hitler is not only a mass murderer, but he beats his pets.) It is the replacement of principled judgment with sentimentality. Ironically, it was this same Nietzchean cult of feeling that "justified" the Fuehrer's sentimentalism. Hitler was genuinely fond of animals, but thought nothing of sending millions of men and women to their deaths.

In contrast with escapist views of human nature, Plutarch once said that all men were endowed "with a lively curiosity and love of knowledge." Therefore, "we ought... to blame the people who abuse these gifts and divert them to objects which are unworthy of attention, while they neglect those which have the best claim to it." A Christian assumes that Adolf Hitler faced the same ethical choices as any man, and could have done good with the talents God gave him. It is only this metaphysical outlook that permits us to understand Hitler without making him a cardboard villain or denying his abilities any more than his malevolence. Unfortunately, Hollywood treats Nazism as the Nazis treated their opponents—inhuman stereotypes unconnected to real life. And so we learn very little about Hitler, or evil.

Christianity and the Pursuit of Leisure

> And what of the opportunity to retire to the society of the best men, and to select some model by which we may direct our own lives? But we can do this only in leisure. — Seneca, *On Leisure*

It may seem that the quest for leisure has become a fetish for us moderns, and the less said of it the better. But Joseph Pieper quickly opens our eyes with the suggestion that our culture does not suffer from the overabundance of leisure but, rather, its scarcity. He would remind us of Aristotle's rather startling assertion that "the first principle of action is leisure." Taking time off from work means more than just bouts of amusement amidst purely utilitarian commotion and toil. Socrates called leisure "the most valuable of possessions," emphasizing that it is the cultivation of the mind for the purpose of fostering and developing virtue.

In a long and productive life that evinced the spiritual repose outlined in *Leisure: The Basis of Culture*, German born Joseph Pieper emerged as an outstanding Catholic thinker of the twentieth century. T. S. Eliot said of him that "however difficult his thought may sometimes be, his sentences are admirably constructed, his ideas expressed with the maximum clarity." As such, Eliot considered Pieper a philosopher who aimed at concision and insight rather than inflated verbiage and obscurantism.

From the outset it is clear that Pieper's appreciation of leisure is at odds with the prevalent view — that it is nothing more than upper-class parasitism (according to writers like Thorstein Veblen, *The Theory of the Leisure Class*). The problem is that most moderns justify every activity according to pragmatic or hedonistic principles. By contrast, Pieper makes a clear distinction between leisure and idleness. The former refers to the contemplative side of man, the ability to passively receive knowledge and wisdom. This same sort of humility is at work when we accept God's grace. In a key phrase, Pieper says that "man seems to mistrust everything that is effortless; he can only enjoy, with a good conscience, what he has acquired with toil and trouble; he refuses to have anything as a gift." By that same token, the contemporary attitude that the goodness of work is directly related to the effort expended is a false one, since St. Thomas Aquinas says the "essence of virtue consists in the good rather than the difficult."

It was Kant and the rationalist intellectuals who began ridiculing the belief that the contemplative life was superior to the active. All virtue, they said, consists in action per se. This reaches the modern existentialist extreme in which any action is "good" simply because it is action. As Sartre believed, "To do something is to create existence." Therein lies the egotistical need to constantly "assert" oneself as if to confirm one's being, whereby even a lewd or criminal act is better than no act at all.

The idea of leisure was transmitted to us from the Greeks. Their word for it, *skole*, also means school. That was because education was time spent in intellectual activity, apart from servile work, which permitted men to contemplate higher things — not just technical learning but inquiry into human society and individual responsibility. For the Christian, this contemplation is given an even greater meaning in prayer. The idea of the Sabbath "and on the seventh day the Lord rested" is an example of how Christianity extended the freedom from servile labor to the entire community. What had been the prerogative of a few free men in a slave-based society eventually became the privilege of all. But it is a privilege that has been undermined by a new paganism which is far less respectful of reflection and contemplation than were the ancients.

Pieper complains of a "proletarianization" that is widespread throughout Capitalist and Socialist societies alike. What he meant by this was quite different from the Marxist definition. A proletarian is one who is totally dedicated to servile work, be it physical or intellectual. Thus while most people assessing their goals in workplace seminars will place personal development ahead of career, their actions tend to belie such claims. Not surprisingly, there are many reasons for the modern worship of labor, which no one today would have the honesty to refer to as servile, since it is a punishment for the sin of Adam. One reason for the supremacy of labor, says Pieper, is the "inner impoverishment of the individual" in secular society who can no longer conceive of anything of value outside the 24/7 paradigm. The only reason for the proletarianized man not working is death.

The fact that Pieper equates religious festivities with leisure gives a better understanding of what the word should mean. He says that "celebration is the core of leisure" which leads us to the further conclusion that "leisure can only be made possible and justifiable on the same basis as the celebration of a festival. That basis is divine worship." He concludes that our modern "holiday" (the contrived festival) cannot compete with the old Holy Days. Since the French Revolution

> attempts have repeatedly been made to manufacture feast days and holidays that have no connection with divine wor-

ship, or are sometimes even opposed to it: 'Brutus days,' or even that hybrid, 'Labour Day.'

St. Thomas says that leisure is not simply a "lack of work." Rather it reflects a spiritual viewpoint that causes a man to accept that there are priorities greater than the ones he sets for himself. According to Pieper, it is a receptive frame attitude of mind and a contemplative attitude that possesses the capacity for "steeping oneself in the whole of creation." For the scholastic philosopher, idleness and the incapacity for leisure correspond with one another. They are the opposite of true leisure and meaningful work.

St. Augustine advised one of his disciples: "I pray thee, spare thyself at times." Pieper could probably say more about the purely practical side of man's need for rest, especially in an age when frenetic entertainment and nerve-racking vacations place their own demands on people's free time. In his classic study *The Intellectual Life*, A.D. Sertillanges, O.P. reminds us that "relaxation is a duty." We need physical rest prior to engaging in active leisure of the intellectual life. Nevertheless, Fr. Sertillanges agrees with Pieper in condemning the false view of "recreation" that allows people just enough time off so that they can climb back on the treadmill with renewed vigor. Mental repose and reflection thereby becomes inferior to the world of "total work." *Leisure: The Basis of Culture* provides a good analogy of why this should not be so:

> [H]owever true it may be that the man who says his nightly prayers sleeps the better for it, nevertheless no one could say his nightly prayers with that in mind. In the same way, no one who looks for leisure simply to restore his working powers will ever discover the fruit of leisure....

In a materialist society there is no room for divine worship or for the feast. The modern world of work reposes upon the principle of "rational utilization." Pieper says there may be "circuses" to supplement the "bread," but such mass entertainment is hardly a true festival. The traditional idea of the festival was one of generosity. In divine worship, there is no calculated return on our time. The same goes for celebrations with friends and family. A world where people refuse to receive (or give) freely is a world lacking in charity. "Cut off from the worship of the divine," says Pieper, "leisure becomes laziness and work inhuman."

When we read about the saints we are struck by their amazing activity. And yet this superabundant activity is counter-balanced by a more salubrious pace of life. One day Bl. Jeanne Jugan, foundress of the Sisters of the Poor, saw a young nun racing pell-mell down a corridor. She brought her to a halt by saying, "You're leaving someone behind you." The Sister turned around and asked, "Excuse me, my good Little Sister, but I can't see anyone..." "Yes, you are. You're leaving God behind. He's letting you run on ahead, for Our Lord... was never in a hurry like you are."

Our intellectual dissipation is rendered easier by technological devices which have invaded even those places that were hitherto safely removed from the noise and temptations of the world. But it would be wrong to make too much of this and posit the blame on external conditions as opposed to internal dispositions. As older spiritual works testify, even the pre-moderns in their bucolic epochs grappled with intellectual distraction, lack of purpose and the neglect of supernatural remedies.

Pieper lays a sound groundwork for the recovery of healthy intellectual life, and we should be inspired to take some concrete steps towards establishing a domestic refuge of Christian *humanitas*. A return to leisure must come about in ways suited to our age and circumstances. It means keeping inane distractions to a reasonable minimum and substituting for them things like reading, learning, creative activities and, most of all, prayer. In this way, all aspects of our life must be transformed—not just in terms of public worship, but also economics, politics, arts and entertainment. In the meantime, a sincere practice of religion will give us a real appreciation of the important things in life, including the idea of leisure.

An Approach to Apologetics

ↄ𝔅

> Christianity is a positive religion, founded on historical facts. While it is true that the beginning, root and foundation of Christianity is faith or acceptance of truths on divine authority, reason provides adequate motives for faith.—Cornelius Hagerty, C.S.C., *The Authenticity of the Sacred Scriptures*

Hilaire Belloc wrote many studies of history from a Catholic perspective. But when reading *The Catholic Church and History* [1] one is pleasantly surprised to discover a work of religious apologetics, albeit one written in Belloc's uniquely terse and commanding style. As such it is not only a solid *defensio fidei*, it also gives us a glimpse into the inspired logic that upheld the author in years of tireless controversy with liberals, Protestants and skeptics. This lucid argumentation will prove just as much an asset to modern readers in confronting anti-Catholic opinion from whatever quarter it may arise.

From the outset, Belloc tells us that a classic apologetic does not consider whether the supernatural teachings of Catholic religion are true, as that is the task of theology. It is, rather, a question whether or not the Church as an entity has always been what it says it is; whether it is consistent or inconsistent in its assertions. As it happens, most criticisms of the faith, from the earliest Christian heresy down to the trendy religious commentary of *Newsweek* magazine, are es-

---

[1] Reprinted by Neumann Press, 2001

sentially arguments "drawn from history." That is why Belloc considers the "negative" task of rebuttal so important.

The author's articulation of fundamentals stands in clear contrast to contemporary discussions of religion which dwell more on vague ethical considerations, social consciousness or group dynamics than the essentials of what the Church is. Belloc sets the terms for the debate by noting that our religion is 1) a unified society under the headship of the Apostolic See of Rome; and 2) it claims to be of divine origin.

According to *The Catholic Church and History* discussion of religion must eliminate impediments on the part of the hearer. Unfortunately this is the first rule that people overlook. It is wrong, says Belloc, to think that we are "trying to prove Catholic truth as one proves a case for a positive verdict." Human reason and philosophy deal with what is *known*; religion and supernatural theology deal with what is *believed*. Belloc's comments are a good refresher in classic Thomism.

> The refutation of any argument against the Faith is not a demonstration of the truth of the Faith. It is the removal only of an obstacle to the Faith. For the Faith is not arrived at by demonstration, but by demonstration it is shown to be at least tenable. The Faith is not a conclusion which all can reach by the formal action of reason, but a revelation to be defended by reason.

The process of proof is one of converging truths rather than simple deduction. Catholic philosopher Etienne Gilson reiterated this fact. "No philosophical speculation can give any necessary reason in favor of any truth" of things like the Trinity, the Incarnation, or the Redemption. These first principles are based on revelation. "Yet, if reason cannot prove them to be true, it cannot either prove them to be false. Quite the reverse" (*Reason and Revelation in the Middle Ages*, 1938). An objective understanding of the past, therefore, does more to substantiate Catholic beliefs than otherwise.

The headache that many encounter is confusion between what the Church officially teaches and the opinions of an individual Catholic cleric or layman. Some views, however much we favor them, are strictly matters of opinion. An individual priest may state that the earth is only 6,000 years old (a point not doctrinally defined), but it is not germane to the discussion of what Catholicism essentially professes. Thus it is only on authoritative and universally binding pronouncements that one may ask whether there is continuity or historical disruption, and not what someone claims the Church has said.

The most impressive aspect of Belloc's study is the way he neatly pre-empts a swarm of anti-Catholic accusations. Without exploring every possible contention, he has done something in just over a hundred pages far more important. He has laid the groundwork for examining charges against our faith based on key principles.

The "historical attack" is divided into two types—the *moral* and *intellectual.* The *moral* argument is of three kinds: 1) the Catholic Church has taught things later proved erroneous, which no Divine Authority would do; 2) the Catholic Church has taught things which were wrong even after being proved wrong; and 3) the Catholic Church is highly and increasingly organized (what we today would call "bureaucratized"), thus demonstrating that it cannot possibly be "spiritual" or of divine origin. Readers will recognize all three as conventional Protestant objections. This last point remains relevant insofar as Catholic modernists have taken up "primitive Christianity" as a chief argument against the "old Church."

The problem, of course, is that the spiritual spontaneity of a never-ending Pentecost exists only in the imagination, not in any historical record. As Belloc wryly remarks, when one eliminates the corporate structure and organization of the Church it leaves us with "no certain source of truth" but only the religious emotion of men which "changes perpetually." Without authority there can be no definition, even of man's basic moral actions. Without hierarchical organization, by which authority is exercised, not even the back-to-basics zealot can make his charge against the organized Church, since he has no foundation for a definitive judgment.

Turning to the *intellectual* arguments against Catholicism, there are two claims to be considered. The first is Protestant, and says that the Catholic Church can be shown to be a mass of man-made accretions resting on an originally genuine basis. The second attack, and the one Belloc considers the most formidable in modern culture, is the "Sceptical or Pagan" argument. It says that the Catholic Church is wholly mythical and just "one more example of man's power of self-delusion."

One of the most prominent (or most tiresome) historical claims against infallibility is the one Belloc sardonically refers to as the "eternal Galileo case." As it turns out, it is the *only* such instance that critics can cite against the Church. Were it not for the fact that Galileo lived in an age of acute theological tension, the affair would have been a tempest in a teapot. It was, notes Belloc, a matter of Church authority and discipline rather than a conflict between scripture and science, since Christians had entertained heliocentric theories as early as John Philoponus in the 7th Century. The

Church authorities simply put Galileo's theory in quarantine to ensure that certain views were not hastily disseminated so as to throw doubt on the inerrancy of the Bible or confuse the unlearned. We take this fact for granted, because no practicing Catholic in the past four hundred years has given the matter a second thought.

There is no disconnect between the faith and the real world, as liberals would have it. Rather, the Church's teaching is confined to essential points on which there is no room for opinion—the fundamental "what" and "why" of creation. It is these things which scientists have never satisfactorily answered, and continue to dispute amongst themselves, as it lies beyond their means. On the other hand, the "how" is left up to specialists to explore in accordance with truly impartial research.

Catholics are not troubled by the specific findings of science, as in the case of Galileo or Darwin, but only by the possible interpretation of those findings. The problem with Darwinism, for example, was taking very limited observation of variations and adaptations within certain species and wildly extrapolating them into a philosophy of the evolutionary origin and development of terrestrial life. Pius XII addressed this question in his encyclical *Humani Generis* (1950). Where too many scientists go wrong is in allowing their studies to be colored with materialistic preconceptions resulting in hypotheses (not proven formulas) resting on false assumptions and, it must be added, lacking in empirical data.

Through Belloc's negative demonstration one also learns what the Church does *not* solemnly teach on such topics. This is relevant in the "Creationism/Evolutionism" debate between Evangelical Protestants and anti-Christian liberals. For us it is not a question of so-called fundamentalism but of authoritative interpretation, without which both the Bible and the propositions of natural reason become meaningless.

On this point we can end where Belloc begins, with a passage that is sublime in its stark logic, because it gets to the heart of Truth itself. In the author's words, the Church always has this to say to man:

> I alone know fully and teach those truths essential to the life of the soul. I alone am that Society wherein the human spirit reposes in its native place; for I alone stand in the centre whence all is seen in proportion and whence the chaotic perspective of things falls into right order. Mankind cannot feed upon itself—for that is death at last. I alone provide external sustenance from that which made mankind. The soil of my country alone can fully nourish mankind. Here, in me, alone is reality. For I alone am not man-made but am of direct divine foundation and am by my divine Founder perpetually maintained.

Here is the timeless challenge that the Church has posed to men of all ages. In the seventy years since *The Catholic Church and History* was written it still remains for the opponents of our religion to contradict it.

The Anthropology of Monotheism

ଓଃ

For well over a century, liberal intellectuals have bullied the common man with anti-religious propaganda. At the heart of their argument is the claim that all spiritual beliefs are a product of social evolution. Our belief in God, the theory goes, grew out of a blind, instinctive impulse and expressed itself in crude forms of worship which developed at a remote point in man's past. This concept is shot through with obvious fallacies. Yet it remains a stock-in-trade argument imposed on students in secular schools, and (since the 1960s) on a growing number of Catholics.

In discussing "comparative religions," evolutionists refer to monotheism, the worship of a single, all-powerful divinity, to distinguish it from polytheism, the worship of multiple divinities as found in pagan cultures. The materialistic development of religions was first popularized by Auguste Comte (1798-1857), the French Positivist thinker. He argued that advanced human cultures had progressed from crude views of divinity, passing through three theological stages-fetishism, polytheism, and monotheism. Needless to say, these stages were not representative of a supernatural reality. They were simply man's imaginative response to inexplicable phenomena of the natural world. Comte's view received further impetus in the last century with James Frazier's popular but inaccurate work, *The Golden Bough*, which is still in print. The idea of "religious progress" has dovetailed nicely with the long-reigning Darwinian views of human physical evolution.

While the polytheism discussed by the older evolutionists ceased to be a factor in Western culture centuries ago, it has seen a resurgence in the form of Wicca and esoteric New Age revivals of primitive cults. Such neo-paganism, however, is artificial and the product not so much of pre-Christian belief as of a reflexive anti-Christianity. In addition to the fad of "primitive" spirituality there are the subtle inaccuracies of "liberal Christianity." This is a heterodox outlook that originated in Protestant circles and worked its way into Catholic thinking in the Twentieth Century. Like the materialists of Comte's school, liberals came to view religion not as an objective link of man to God, but as an ever changing subjective "relationship" which is developing and, in some vague way, progressing towards gradual perfection. Even if the liberal admits to the existence of a Creator, man's relationship with Him is distant enough to render dogma unnecessary. In that sense, the religious evolutionary argument is a convenient postscript for the individual who lacks moral and doctrinal precision (yet prefers the emotional comforts of belonging to a "church").

In contrast with this sort of guesswork, objective scientific study indicates that polytheism—as found in socially advanced cultures like Greece and Rome—was not an early stage of human development at all, but a degeneration of man's earliest religious beliefs. An "original revelation" was handed down from Adam and thence passed on by Noah to his descendents after the Deluge. Monotheism is thus natural to man, while polytheism represents a spiritual and moral corruption as people gradually turned away from God's teachings. By the time of the first written records, all peoples, with the exception of the Hebrews, had lapsed into false views of the Divinity. However, remnants of the original revelation were to be found in isolated primitive tribes scattered across the globe, some of whom maintained fairly unspoiled monotheistic practices until modern times. It is the thorough documentation of these practices which forms the scientific rebuttal of evolutionist claims.

Catholic scholar Christopher Dawson identifies the three main influences which form and modify human culture: genetics, environment, and function or occupation. "But in addition to these there is a fourth element...which is peculiar to the human species and the existence of which frees man from the blind dependence on material environment which characterises the lower forms of life."[1] He is referring to human thought, which manifests itself in its highest and most revealing form in religion. That leads us to the definition of religion itself. Dawson insists on precision, and is not satisfied with such hazy descriptions as the "worship of natural forces" or even a "belief in spiritual beings." Rather, he says that wherever "man has a sense of dependence on external powers which are conceived as mysterious and higher than man's own, there is religion, and the feelings of awe and self-abasement with which man is filled in the presence of such powers is essentially a religious emotion, the root of worship and prayer."[2] This worship is based on belief in an objective supernatural reality.

By contrast, Comte claimed that examples of man's earliest religious ideas was to be found by examining the fetish-worship of the African tribes. In order to understand the development of humanity one therefore had to start with examples of men at the most primitive level. Catholic histo-

---

[1] Christopher Dawson, *The Age of the Gods*, 1928, p. xvi.

[2] Ibid, p. 22.

rian John T. Driscoll replied that Comte's "argument can be inverted. For if the customs of savages may be found among civilized races, evident traces of higher ideals are also found among savages."[3] That is the starting point for the reasoned refutation of materialistic religious development.

Our knowledge of the thought and religious life of the earliest men can be derived from two sources: 1) the religion of contemporary primitives, as observed by ethnology and cultural anthropology; and 2) correlation of these facts with evidence of absolute primitives, discovered by the first European explorers, and as later found in prehistoric remains.

Study of contemporary primitives reveals one undeniable fact. Atheism is not a natural condition in any race or tribe of mankind. It very literally has to be beaten into people, as it was in Communist Russia. On the contrary, every people has historically followed some religion. It is further documented that the more primitive the group, the more pure the religious dimension tends to be. Dawson says that the hunter-gatherers

> are in no sense pre-religious or a-religious. They are on the contrary more religious than the peoples of the higher cultures, since the essential religious attitude—the sense of dependence on mysterious external powers—is stronger with them than it is in the case of civilised societies.[4]

While the accidentals (names, linguistic conventions, etc.) vary from tribe to tribe, all hunter-gatherers essentially practice the same religion. What is more astonishing is that these groups are scattered in remote areas and thus have no contact with one another. This dispersed world-wide unity

---

[3] John T. Driscoll, "Fetishism," *Catholic Encyclopedia*, Vol. VI, 1911.

[4] Dawson, p. 26.

suggests that common religious concepts are derived from a common origin. Study of these tribes reveals interesting points. First, their religion is qualitatively high in its tenets. Second, despite their lack of economic and social development, their religion is fully interwoven with their mundane tasks. The primitives do not limit themselves to the practices of earthly living only. They practice their religion and hand it on formatively to their children. In fact, their belief is central to the individual's passage from childhood to adolescence to adulthood. Rather than displaying a cleavage between spiritual belief and daily life, the religion of the hunter-gatherer gives meaning to all that they do.

The archaeological remains of the Neanderthal show that even the earliest man practiced intricate burial rituals. They certainly believed in an afterlife. Likewise, sacrifice as a mode of worship amongst primitives is ubiquitous. Being food-gatherers they consider whatever edibles they find as something provided by their Heavenly Father. Custom, having the force of religious law, compels them to offer the first portion to their Provider. Contrary to the idealized nature-worship as misconstrued by modern secular anthropology, such primitives acknowledge their dependence on nature but at the same time it is seen as something "partly external and foreign." Indeed, Dawson explains, such hunters do not single out natural forces to be worshipped as do the more advanced pagan peoples. They comprehend a universal force behind nature. For example, the Tlingit Indians of Alaska see the Supreme Being as a pure spirit who knows all things.

As the same time that Comte and other evolutionists were theorizing *ex nihilo*, an English contemporary was actually recording what he saw while living among the primitives of Oceania. Edward Horace Mann, a British government employee, was appointed colonial administrator of the Andaman Islands in 1858. Taking the time to master the native tongue of the aborigines, Mann published a grammar and vocabulary. Following his retirement and return to England, he wrote *The Aboriginal Inhabitants of the Andaman Islands* (printed by the Royal Anthropological Institute in 1885). The book received generous accolades for its scientific detail. Among other things, Mann found among the Andamese

> knowledge of, or belief in, a Supreme Being, whom they call Puluga. Of him they say that he is invisible, was never born and is immortal, and that by him the world and all objects, animate or inanimate, were created, excepting only the powers of evil. He is regarded as omniscient... and is angered by the commission of certain sins.[5]

The Oceanian aborigines were found to have had more than merely vague intimations of immortality. They believed that this Supreme Being "is the Judge from whom each soul receives its sentence after death."[6]

> At the resurrection they will be reunited and live permanently on the new earth... All will then remain in the prime of life, sickness and death will be unknown, and there will be no more marrying or giving in marriage. The animals, birds and fish will also reappear in the new world in their present form. This blissful state will be inaugurated by a great earthquake, occurring by Puluga's command... There is no trace to be found of the worship of trees, stones or other objects, and it is a mistake to suppose that they adore or invoke celestial bodies... No reason is given for the formation of the earth's surface, except that it was according to the will of Puluga, the creator of all.[7]

---

[5] Edward Horace Mann, *The Aboriginal Inhabitants of the Andaman Islands*, p. 89.

[6] Ibid, p. 90.

[7] Ibid, pp. 94-5.

From his knowledge of Andaman culture and their marked resistance to foreigners, Mann judged it improbable that their legends were the corrupted product of interaction with Christian missionaries. At the same time, it is the missionaries who have left us with invaluable records of primitive peoples and their beliefs. A more recent account from another part of the world is provided by Fr. E. de Viron, a Catholic priest who operated a parish in Ngoma in Rwanda. One of the groups in that country are the Pygmies. While superficial observers, like tourists on safari or graduate students on field trips, see only obvious corruptions like the "cult of the dead" and "mystical relations with spirits," Fr. de Viron examined the Pygmy beliefs more deeply, finding consistent belief in a transcendent God called "Immana."

The primitive monotheist and the Christian alike see the phenomena of nature as God's creatures. On the other hand, where the light of revelation was obscured in whole or in part, people tended to deify things, such as the Moon and stars (lacking advanced scientific knowledge to explain the laws of nature). Polytheistic nature-worship is the mistaken application of a sound principle, an awareness of a mind or will behind the actions of the world around us. Even in polytheism there is an indication of a spontaneous religious sense which cannot be explained away by contemporary philosophy. The error of polytheism, however, lies in the fragmenting of that Will, which is found in all the operations of nature, into a plurality of divinities, each active and dominant within a province of its own. *The Catholic Encyclopedia* offers this summary:

> Polytheistic nature-worship is to be found among practically all peoples who have lacked the guiding star of Divine revelation. Such history of these individual religions... offers little

> evidence of an upward development towards Monotheism: on the contrary, in almost every instance of known historic development, the tendency has been to degenerate further and further from the monotheistic idea. There is, indeed, scarcely a Polytheistic religion in which one of the many deities recognized is not held in honour as the father and lord of the rest...[8]

The ancient Chinese religion was remarkably close to pure Monotheism. By contrast, the crude nature-worship of the Egyptians of later times was decidedly a corruption of quasi-Monotheistic beliefs while the Vedic religion of India later deteriorated into outright pantheism.

The examples of Mann and de Viron noted above are just a few of the many instructive reports published in the last century or so. Even agnostic writers, unable to ignore hard evidence, attest to the problems with the popular evolutionary hypothesis. Speaking of the evidence of early monotheism, *The Religious Experience of Mankind* (1969) admits to

> a reversal of the usual position of those who have been influenced by evolutionary theory, who tend to equate 'later' religion with 'higher' religion, and who regard monotheism as the highest development of all... In any event it is a striking fact that many primitive cultures have a belief in some sort of High God...[9]

Such works acknowledge the tendency of primitives to maintain their monotheism in a more pure and elevated state, less mixed with the later growth of idolatry, magic and superstition. Monotheism characterizes the beliefs of food-gatherers, whereas deviant and degrading practices, such as

---

[8] Chales F. Aiken, "Monotheism," *Catholic Encyclopedia*, Vol. X, 1911; for a more in-depth Catholic study see Fr. Wilhelm Schmidt, *The Origin and Growth of Religion*, 1931.

[9] Ninian Smart, *The Religious Experience of Mankind*, 1969, p.53.

human sacrifice and ritual perversion, are observed to have set in among the food-producers. Ironically, it is the primitives who are closer than the polytheists to the first tenet of religion in rendering homage to the Heavenly Father. "The most popular prayer in the world is addressed to 'Our Father who art in heaven'," says Mircea Eliade.[10] It is also interesting to see how primitive accounts of Creation show clear parallels to the Book of Genesis. "The existence of such conceptions among folk as far apart as the inhabitants of Tierra del Fuego [at the Southern end of Chile] and the Arctic is a significant indication that primitive religion... possesses sophisticated ideas about the beginning and creation of the world, and about a supreme architect of the world."[11] Such similarities cannot be easily written off as the happy coincidence of naturalistic development.

The religious evolution argument is increasingly challenged on an empirical level by objective anthropological and archaeological study, though it is still disseminated in a "popular" philosophical format. An example of this is the highly publicized *Power of Myth* series by pantheist Joseph Campbell. Nevertheless, careful correlation of ethnological and archaeological data makes it possible to ascertain a remnant of "original revelation," as given to our First Parents, and to explode the stale but persistent hypothesis put forth by Comte over a century and a half ago.

---

[10] Mircea Eliade, *Patterns in Comparative Religion*, 1958, p.38.

[11] Smart, p.55.

The Psychology of Unbelief

☙

> The great psychologists of the ages have universally agreed that the root of all unhappiness is selfishness or egotism. Egotism is the rejection of the double command to love God and neighbor, and the affirmation of the self as the standard of all truth and morality.—Fulton Sheen, *The Way to Happiness*

To discuss religious commitment from a psychological viewpoint is not to imply that faith or moral choices are shaped entirely by external things like environment, body chemistry or sensory stimuli. If we remain true to psychology's origins, beginning with Aristotle, we approach it as a branch of metaphysics which studies the life of the soul. At the same time, classical psychology (as opposed to idealism), does not dismiss the importance of physical reality. A whole range of factors can influence one's mental behavior—including social relations, physical health, economic status, etc.—while leaving man's free will fundamentally intact. Unfortunately, with the changes in epistemology and ethics growing out of the so-called Enlightenment, psychological commentators veered away from the Western tradition.

The American William James, for example, applied Darwin's evolutionary hypothesis to the development of the human consciousness in *The Principles of Psychology* (1890). A short while later, Sigmund Freud articulated the belief that human behavior was shaped by early life influences and the tendency to repress desires. Sexual drives were also seen as a key determinant in individual choices. While Freud was understandably reacting to the hyper-rationalism of earlier secularists (who denied the irrational side of fallen humanity), his theories further displaced belief in objective and transcendent morality.

Christian psychology, by contrast, should help one to understand the behavioral characteristics of the individual within an ethical framework. Recalling psychology's Aristotelian roots, one can make the connection between repeated choices ("ethics" is from the Greek word *ethos*, meaning "custom" or "habit") and the patterns of mental activity which emerge from consistent preferences in one direction or another. While the operations of the mind do not determine morality, the two react upon and shape one another. For example, distinct patterns have been clinically observed in people suffering from extremely violent tendencies. As Sheen puts it, a man's "secret hates, his hidden sins, his flippant treading upon the laws of morality—all of these leave their traces in his mind, his heart and his unconsciousness."

Helpful to a Catholic understanding of the subject is Dr. Paul C. Vitz's *Faith of the Fatherless: The Psychology of Atheism.* Dr. Vitz, a scholar and convert, states that historically important atheists "are the product of their historical period, family psychology (that is, the defective father), intellectual intelligence and level of ambition, and—last but far from least—their own free choice." Such findings, based on decades of research as a psychologist, flout materialistic views that the idea of God is simply a "projection theory" based on man's need for security.

For Freud and others, religion could be criticized on the basis of believers' supposedly subjective motives. Vitz boldly reverses this paradigm. Atheism is not so aloof as it pretends to be, and is as susceptible as any other attitude to external factors. Vitz makes his point by considering the lives of dozens of major atheists and seeing what they might have in common. It transpires that, almost without exception, militant skeptics of the last two centuries, from Voltaire to Stalin, have suffered from a "defective father"—one who was absent through death or through moral failure. As a result, the stance taken by leading atheists may be seen (at least in part) as an emotional reaction against paternal figures, including the divine Father.

Much has been written about the absence of fathers in modern families. "Presumably," remarks Vitz, "this widespread defective fathering will cause an increase in contemporary skeptical attitudes towards God. But it may also result in an equally widespread 'father hunger' which could manifest itself in a variety of ways, such as a growth in cults and support for political demagogues." It is also worth noting, with regard to the unprecedented explosion of moral deviancy since the 1960s, that homosexuals tend to suffer from hostile or absent fathers, leading to "defensive detachment" from the father and other males. If anything, it shows that Vitz's thesis applies to a wide range of contemporary dysfunctional behavior and apostasy. Speaking of the decline of Christianity, he makes a point concerning the sudden vogue of black American males converting to Islam:

> Recently I heard a report that black Baptist women were urging their husbands to become Muslims because they thought their men should have a religion and thought Christianity to be inadequate for men. The African-American community has suffered greatly from fatherless families, and many blacks who have become Muslims openly claim that Islam restored their manhood to them ("The Father Almighty, Maker of Male & Female," *Touchstone*, January/February, 2001).

In this case, the attraction of Islam is due to a lack of emphasis on fatherhood in the black urban community and in Christianity at large. Men eager to assert their traditional role are left without spiritual support. This has been most evident in liberal, mainstream Protestant denominations where feminist and androgynous "unisex" theology has been heavily promoted.

As for widespread theoretical atheism, it is a relatively new phenomenon. Vitz believes that atheism, rather than traditional theism, is a social construct, and one prone to changing habits and tastes. While environmental influences do not determine unbelief, the social milieu can predispose people to a particular way of expressing their moral and theological rebellion. It happens that since the late 17th century, explicit skepticism has been the most convenient and acceptable outlet. As Samuel Johnson said of the libertine poet, the Earl of Rochester: "He lost all sense of religious restraint, and finding it not convenient to admit the authority of laws which he resolved not to obey, sheltered his wickedness behind infidelity."

An atheist's upbringing is revealing. Even more so is his high level of egotism. "Nietzche's pride and his arrogance," observes Vitz, "often to the point of pathos, are widely acknowledged." The same was true of Ludwig Feuerbach, H. G. Wells, Bertrand Russell and Adolf Hitler. In his other recent book, *Psychology as Religion: The Cult of Self-Worship*, Dr. Vitz discusses the problem of selfism or "self theory," which is liberal psychology's rationalization of egocentrism. It is "an example of a horizontal heresy, with its emphasis on the present and on self-centered ethics." As such it manifests itself in as many guises as egotism is capable of: materialist sociology, group therapy, New Age movements, or the "power of positive thinking" Protestant sects. At the root of this is metaphysical denial.

"A final profound conflict between Christianity and selfism," Vitz explains, "centers around the meaning of suffering. The Christian acknowledges evil... as a fact of life." Christianity accepts the existence of sin and death. It also provides a way to transcend and transform them. "In contrast, selfist philosophy trivializes life by claiming that suffering (and, by implication, even death) is without intrinsic meaning. Suffering is seen as some sort of absurdity, usually a man-made mistake that could have been avoided by use of knowledge to gain control of the environment." Evil is thus externalized, or removed from the realm of personal moral culpability. It is the predictable operation of pride. We tend to credit success to ourselves while blaming our failures on others.

Heterodox philosophies not only appeal to man's baser instincts, they "validate" them. False theology is an expedient rationalization for antinomian behavior, which eschews moral responsibility. Nevertheless, one must keep in mind that along with obdurate heretics are misguided individuals, who may be attracted to some residual good in a false system (since no belief is absolutely evil; its error lies in subordinating higher goods to lesser ones). Catholic theologians tell us that where there is unconscious ignorance of Church teaching, erroneous judgment, and imperfect comprehension, a necessary condition of sinfulness—free choice—is lacking. With this in mind, apologetics need to be conducted with prudence as well as conviction. Like the wheat and tares in the parable, it is difficult for us to hastily root up the outwardly bad without causing undue mischief.

Msgr. Ronald Knox, who addressed psychological problems in his sermons and essays, provides further insights. He rephrased the skeptic's taunt that "man creates God in his own image," observing that when "turning your thoughts toward the Supreme, the Ultimate, you can choose, evidently, this or that aspect, this or that avenue or approach." St. Augustine argued much the same point in his *Catechetical Instruction.* Awareness on the part of the religious instructor of the catechumen's fears, dislikes, and even his physical comfort is not inconsequential. Augustine's psychological view of conversion has been reiterated by later apologists. We are taught not to mistake our own temperament, preferences or fashions for an objective standard. Related to this is another point raised by Vitz; namely, that religion is the solution but, superficially, it can sometimes be the problem. In this sense, the believer sees sanctimonious behavior as the failure of the individual to live up to God's calling, while the non-believer feels it shows up religion for the "falsehood" that it is. There is no denying the scandal of religious hypocrisy. It is important to acknowledge this point in dealing with the sincere individual who has experienced such failings. It can be a mitigating, if not justifying, factor in his momentary rejection of faith.

Religious hypocrisy goes beyond everyday human frailties. As an example of this, Vitz discusses Søren Kierkegaard's father who was an austere and sometimes troubled man who nevertheless displayed genuine piety, compunction and love. He eventually earned his son's affection. The younger Kierkegaard was also a devoted Christian who overcame tremendous temptations to doubt, and even displayed a marked sympathy to Catholic thinking towards the end of his life. In stark contrast is the pitiable conduct of Jacob Freud, father of the psychoanalyst, who was not only cowardly and incompetent, but a pervert and pedophile. Says Vitz: "in proposing the Oedipus complex, Freud placed hatred of the father at the center of his psychology." There was a very real basis for supposing that this expressed "his strong unconscious hostility to and rejection of his father." What surely enhanced Sigmund's distaste for religion was that Jacob carried on as an outwardly proper and observant Jew who spent long hours on readings and devotions. Needless to say, double standards are not unique to Judaism. Dr. Vitz gives examples of individuals raised in lax or rigorist Christian circumstances who, sadly, turned on their faith.

Vitz leaves us with an interesting paradox. Psychology will never be a proper yardstick for measuring the truth or falsity of religion. *Faith of the Fatherless* favors "the premodern idea that controversies should be settled on the basis of the evidence, not on the psychology of the interlocutors. In this framework, *ad hominem* arguments must be rejected as irrelevant—and all psychological arguments are *ad hominem*; that is, they address the person presenting the evidence and not the evidence itself." At the same time, psychological understanding is important as a prelude to apologetics. It helps us to appreciate the motives for a person's unbelief, which may include some intense, personal trauma.

> If one wishes to genuinely reach such people, one must address their underlying psychology. Aside from the common, superficial reasons, most serious unbelievers are likely to have painful memories underlying their rationalization of atheism. Such interior wounds... need to be fully appreciated and addressed by believers.

Philosophy and the Early Church

If the classic triad of the Good, the True, and the Beautiful, as championed by Socrates, comes from God, then nothing of value is to be disdained in man's spiritual quest. As St. Paul observed: "Jews want miracles for proof, and Greeks look for wisdom" (I Cor. 1:23). Even two thousand years later converts to the faith tend to follow one of these separate but converging paths to truth. Nor is it necessary to univocally reject one approach for another.

For those coming from a prior religious background, the chief hurdle lies in accepting the proofs of Catholic claims to authority and authenticity. At the other end of the spectrum are the converts from rationalism who must accept the very fundamentals of the supernatural life. These are the souls, described by Dominican theologian Fr. Garrigou-Lagrange, who are "dominated by the intellect" and "climb the mountain by another path." The philosopher or seeker of wisdom is a member of this group—men like St. Justin Martyr (100-165). St. Justin was a Syrian Greek who studied Platonism before receiving baptism at age 38 and frequently cited pre-Christian thinkers in his apologetic works.

While Christian civilization stands out for its fostering of a centuries-long collaboration between philosophy and religion, there have been moments of friction and misunderstanding. As French Thomist Etienne Gilson explains, some have always opposed philosophy *per se*, or held it to be deeply suspect, among them the brilliant but rigorist (and ultimately heretical) Tertullian (c. 160-230). Yet the main trend has been more positive. When considering, for example, the career of St. Augustine (354-430) it would be difficult to decide which trait was more in evidence, the poignant devotion and introspection of *The Confessions* or the erudite rhetoric and analysis of *The City of God.* Considered objectively, the mystical and the rational are complementary, not contradictory. Thus, while some early Christians held philosophy in suspicion, Justin Martyr understood it *not* in the sense that most people (then and now) think of it, as merely the opinions of a particular school—which is due to the misuse rather than the proper use of philosophy—but as the realization of what is true and helpful to man. He did it high honor when he said, "I find this philosophy [Christianity] alone to be sure and profitable" (*Dialogue with Trypho*, 8). Likewise, the early Bishop Melito of Tardis referred to the faith as "our philosophy."

Speaking of the important writings of the early Christian historian Eusebius (260-339), Andrew Louth says: "The appeal to philosophy, especially to Platonism, and the claim that Christianity was vindicated by what was best in the philosophers, coupled with the claim that Christianity, through its link to Judaism, was the oldest of all religions, are the parts of this apologetic tradition that most appealed to Eusebius" (Introduction, *The History of the Church*, Penguin Books).

We can infer from the Epistles of St. Paul that, as the Church's first theologian, he was familiar with the philosophical arguments of his day. The former Pharisee from Tarsus was an educated man and well-read in the nobler sages of Greco-Roman culture, as revealed in his allusion in the Epistles to thinkers like Epimenides and Aratus, while in

I Corinthians he quotes Menander's saying that "Evil communications corrupt good manners."

While addressing the Stoics and Epicureans of Athens, the Apostle speaks to them of the "unknown god" which they had venerated by means of natural theology. In so doing, he acknowledged that there was a passable bridge to the faith by means of wisdom and virtue, if men were humble enough to cross it. Similarly, in one of his best-known passages, the Apostle acknowledges the law written on men's hearts (Rom 2:15). Such a phrase would have been immediately comprehensible to Seneca (the Stoic philosopher and contemporary of St. Paul) as "nature" or the "law of nature." It is important to note that this was not the naturalism of later skeptics, but what Catholic philosophers defined as the *natural law*—those truths observable by ordinary means in the contemplation of the order of God's creation.

According to the natural law, human reason sees that there must be a subordination of the lower needs to the higher so as to maintain harmony amongst our conflicting desires and tendencies. Cicero, in the century before Christ's birth, enunciated the natural law by describing truths that stood apart from the mere opinions of time or locality, and thus applied to all men:

> The law is right reason in agreement with nature, worldwide in scope, unchanging, everlasting.... We may not oppose or alter that law, we cannot abolish it, we cannot be freed from its obligations by any legislature.... This law does not differ for Rome and for Athens, for the present and for the future.... He who disobeys it denies himself and his own nature.

With the fall of the Greek city states and the rise of empire (first that of Alexander and later of Rome) there was a sense that universalism must overcome particularism, especially in ethics. Even the gifted Aristotle, who gave us the systematized study of moral philosophy, was hampered by the parochialism of the city state and the belief that some men were "slaves by nature." By contrast, the new school of Stoicism believed in the universal brotherhood of man and was strongly critical of slavery, human blood sports and even (as in the writings of Epictetus) the horrible practice of infanticide. The Stoics, whom Cicero admired, were instrumental in fostering an outlook that recognized the moral worth, and responsibility, of all men. As such, they strove against many of the vices and immoral pastimes of the ancient world.

It comes as little surprise that learned Christians, steeped in the literature of Greece and Rome, employed the arguments of pagans even against pagans. For, as Seneca said when quoting a rival, "Whatever is true is my property." The use of virtuous non-Christian writings, like the use of the Roman basilica design for the early places of worship, was a natural development. But it may also have been a conscious effort on the part of Christian thinkers to speak in terms familiar to the Gentiles, just as apologists today relate timeless truths in an idiom that their audience can readily understand and sympathize with.

St. Jerome (c. 340-420), in his letter to Marcus, a Roman orator, wanted to help his friend overcome scruples about studying pagan authors. Jerome reminded him of the philosophical learning employed by early witnesses of the faith, like Bishop Quadratus, Aristides and Justin Martyr, all of whom presented learned apologetics to the Roman Emperor. He says that most of the works of the ancients, with the exception of the obvious hedonists, "are extremely full of erudition and philosophy [love of wisdom]" (Letter LXX).

Another Father of the Eastern Church, St. Basil the Great (329-379), echoed these sentiments in his "Address to Young Men on Reading Greek Literature," which remains a valuable reference for all students of literature. He tells his readers that "pagan learning is not without usefulness for the soul." Further:

> almost all of the writers who have some reputation for wisdom have, to a greater or lesser degree, each to the best of his power, discoursed in their works in praise of virtue. To these men we must hearken and we must try to show forth their words in our lives; for he in truth who confirms by act his devotion to wisdom, which among others is confined to words, "he alone has understanding, but the others flit about as shadows."

The convergence of philosophy and religion was not coincidental. Rather, this fruitful meeting of natural and supernatural thought was purposefully ordained by an Eternal Providence in the gradual unfolding of history. What we have come to know as the Christian West was formed by the confluence of the three great cultures of the ancient world: the Hebrews, from whom we derived our religion; the Greeks, who gave us philosophy; and the Romans, who provided legal and political order. Men like David, Socrates and Cicero could be taken as the respective archetypes of these cultures. Nor was there lacking a representative of the new spiritual order. The triune cultural foundation of Christianity was perfectly reflected in the life of St. Paul, a Roman citizen and a Jew of Greek learning.

In reviewing pagan writings leading up to the birth of Christ, it is interesting to see in the nobler Greek thinkers a form of sincere, if obviously limited, "mysticism" that may have helped the better among them to appreciate Jewish (and later Christian) spirituality. "If Plato," writes St. Augustine, "says that the wise man is the man who imitates, knows and loves this God… what need is there to examine the other philosophers? There are none who come nearer to us than the Platonists" (*City of God*, VIII, 5).

The Bishop of Hippo pays tribute to a philosophy which had rescued him from the grotesque errors of the Manichees. St. Jerome offers similar praise for Plato in contrasting the mere sophist or rhetorician, who puts on a show of learning, with the genuine student of wisdom:

> [O]ne will say, quoting Euripides, "the tongue has sworn, but the mind is unsworn," and the appearance of being good will be his aim instead of being good. Yet this is the last extreme of injustice, if we are to hearken to the words of Plato—"to appear to be just without being so."

While some of Plato's theories lacked the realism of later thinkers, as for example in his utopian *Republic*, his ethics were an admirable development while his metaphysics became a watershed for classical thought. "When we say that God created and arranged all things in this world," remarks St. Justin, "we seem to repeat the teachings of Plato" (Apol. 1.20). This is a reference to the creation myth of the *Timeas*. Plato was unlike other pre-Christians (including his student Aristotle), who believed in the eternity of the world. When discussing the existence of the soul's immortality in his dialogue *Phaedo*, it is clearly as much an article of faith for the Greek thinker as it is an attempt at logical inference of spiritual truths.

Following in this tradition, the neo-Platonist Philo (c. 20 B.C. – A.D. 50) said that reason broke down beyond a certain limit, at which point it was given a "revelation of the Deity by the *Logos*." As it turns out, Philo was a Jew, and an example of how the Platonic and Hebraic worldviews, seemingly incompatible on one level, were brought into fruitful contact through Hellenization—the cultural transformation of the Near East through the conquests of Alexander the Great. According to Eusebius, "Philo became widely known as one of the greatest scholars, not only among [the Christians] but also among those brought up as pagans" (*History of the Church*, I.4). This Hebrew polymath wrote prolific commentaries on Jewish Scriptures as well as philosophical works, which were attractive to Christian theologians from the time of St. Clement (first century) to Ss. Ambrose and Gregory (fourth century).

Philo's works were preserved by Christians given the affinity between his writings and many points of the new creed. Following in the footsteps of Philo, an apologist such as St. Justin Martyr could more readily draw comparisons between the pre-Christian notion of *logos*, which dimly perceived the transcendent Truth behind Creation, and the *Logos* (the Word of God) for his pagan audiences. "Everything that the philosophers and legislators discovered and expressed well, they accomplished through their discovery and contemplation of some part of the *logos*" (Apol. 2.10). In this sense, the *logos* was that Wisdom which God had implanted in us, referring both to Cicero's law of nature and St. Paul's law written on the hearts of men.

It is clear that the search for truth and meaning on a natural level is fulfilled, not contradicted, by Divine Revelation. By that same token, Revelation does not replace logic or eliminate the need for using our heads. While there is much in our religion that is beyond the limited understanding of human reason (this is true even of many observable phenomena in creation), it is not on that account irrational, but super-rational. The wiser pre-Christian sages made room for this element of faith. In Plato's dialogue *Phaedrus*, Socrates speaks of a "divine sign" which leads him in his search for truth. He says that the "soul itself is endowed with some power of divination," and beyond reason is a "divine madness" or inspiration and prophecy inspired by God. Elsewhere, Socrates speaks of "divine possession" and "heavenly vision."

If the pagans possessed many vices, they also had many virtues which we in our cultural retrogression seem to be quickly shedding. Garrigrou-Lagrange noted that where faith degenerates it "becomes the principle of a false mysticism," and even superstition, which is far worse than invincible ignorance of Christianity. Ironically, by rejecting the supernatural, men come to abandon the natural values, including the Greco-Roman ideal of moral and intellectual excellence. "When men abandoned the Christian truth, their fall was accelerated by the height from which they fell." By contrast, classic antiquity "was not afflicted by such complete lack of equilibrium." The nobler aspects of ancient civilization formed a solid foundation ready for the "elevation of the Gospel."

The different "roles" of philosophy and religion are collaborative rather than exclusive, in the way that up-to-date biology does not supplant Church teaching on certain moral issues, but helps expand our appreciation, and aid our explanation, of those beliefs. Just as the development of Greco-Roman civilization, in the eyes of St. Augustine, was a proximate preparation for the Incarnation, so the intellectual life of a culture is important in aiding (or hindering) the reception of the Gospel. In that respect, all that is good in philosophy not only has God's blessing, but has Him as it Source and Author.

As the popular philosopher and convert Mortimer Adler explained, philosophy has reality as its object. Our senses serve reason, which reflects upon and seeks to understand known facts. Religion's object, by contrast, is ultimate mysteries. Its method is receptive. Yet reason has its role even in relation to Revelation. It accepts and believes what is given to it. A good example of philosophy acting as the "handmaid of faith" is the way in which Platonist concepts, especially those of Plotinus (whom St. Augustine studied) underlie the profound explanations of Christian theology in discussing the nature of God, eternity and spiritual being.

The modern reader will also note the unmistakable contrast between modern intellectualism and the classical works studied by the Church Fathers. The "philosophies" of our time are really variations on the theme of self-justification. From Thomas Hobbes to Rousseau, from J. S. Mill to Bertrand Russell, we have witnessed one long exercise in situation ethics, by which men force the ideal to fit their own conduct and not men to fit the ideal. The realist philosophers of the past, by contrast, sought to appreciate objective truth and help man conform to it. While the erroneous schools of the Sophists, Cynics and Skeptics wielded some influence, they were chiefly a distraction from the main intellectual current of the Platonists, the Peripatetics, and the Stoics. Even the original Epicureans, it should be noted, were austere and disciplined in their search for mental repose as compared to their hedonistic modern counterparts, for whom any self-denial is a negation of their pursuit of pleasure.

The *philosophia perennis* (perennial philosophy) is the classical wisdom that forms a continuous thread from the time of Socrates to that Christian devotee of ancient learning, Boethius (480-524). St. Augustine's own life is testimony to the fact that the study of great works in the realist tradition can inoculate one against false ideas. He tells us in the *Confessions* that Cicero's *Hortensius* helped him to place wisdom and the pursuit of truth above the purely rhetorical studies that hitherto preoccupied him. Yet Augustine would also point out that the Christian has an advantage over the non-Christian in not only appreciating philosophy's strengths, but also its limits. None of the intellectual schools, however brilliant, represent unassailable dogma. It is only comparatively late in human history that ideas have attempted the hegemony of the all-embracing "-ism," which feels it must substitute something for the certitudes of faith it has replaced.

On a Christian level, Augustine was deeply indebted to Platonic thought, though he was not, strictly speaking, a "Platonist" any more than Aquinas, who culled much from Aristotle, was an "Aristotelian." Indeed, St. Thomas was actually combating pure Aristotelianism (Averroism by way of the Muslim world) which was threatening Catholic philosophy with pantheistic and skeptical ideas.

It is primarily in the study of ethics—the science of right conduct—that non-Christian wisdom can be an aid to the believer. The similarities between pagan mores and Christian ethics provide an impartial refutation of claims that our religion's dictates are somehow unnatural or lacking in common sense. Consider how some of the great maxims of Christianity are echoed in the writings of the sages:

> "It is better to give than to receive" (Aristotle).

> "If I had to choose between doing wrong and having wrong done to me, I'd prefer the latter" (Socrates).

> "I regard God's will as better than my will. I shall attach myself to him as a servant and follower" (Epictetus).

At the same time we quickly realize that the heroic adherents of pre-Christian philosophy were insignificant compared to the thousands of saints who have won recognition for their holiness even by those outside the Church. The pagan world could not live up to its own best ideals. Nor could its leading thinkers overcome their perplexity at the persistent irrationality behind human behavior.

Aristotle, in the *Nichomachean Ethics*, analyzed moral conduct and the personal responsibility for bad actions. Yet he could not account for the manner in which man's flawed nature—his tendency to evil—came about. Likewise, Seneca seemed to admit the woeful inadequacy of humanist "self-sufficiency" by his repeated endorsement of suicide as the way of escaping from life's greatest hardships. As the late Thomist Dr. Frederick Wilhelmsen said rather pointedly: "Our Christian hero cannot be the pagan Socrates. He only uttered a number of questions the answers to which have been known by every youngster educated in Christendom for decades of centuries."

But it is not that philosophy is downgraded by the appearance of the faith. Rather, the moral quest of the ancients ceased to be confined to a learned few and became the province of *all* men. In that sense, philosophy is both subordinated to and ennobled by the higher revealed truths of God. Historian Robert L. Wilken aptly summarizes the harmonious relationship which was as beneficial to philosophy as it was helpful to religion:

> Christianity set a new agenda for philosophers. The distinctive traits of the new religion and the tenacity of Christian apologists in defending their faith opened up new horizons for Greco-Roman culture and breathed new life into the

spiritual and intellectual traditions of the ancient world (*The Christians as the Romans Saw Them*).

God and History

Three centuries before Christ, the Greek poet Cleanthes said "naught upon Earth is wrought in thy despite, O God." Wherever we look, belief in a superior power ruling over the universe has been the norm in every civilization prior to the secular societies of the modern era. Unfortunately most Westerners, even self-professed Christians, tend to think in terms of divine aloofness rather than God's active intervention, being embarrassed into this view by their peers in the media and academia.

To treat history as if "God mattered" is to get beyond the superficial and the obvious; the clutter of mere opinions and trivia about the past. A religious view of history is not, however, another form of ivory tower idealism. On the contrary, the problems of contemporary society make more sense as we approach them from a well-ordered Christian perspective. This perspective demands taking into account both the grand sweep of events as well as the small details. The big picture gives us a sense of direction, while observation of precise data confirms the larger truths or acts as a corrective for false constructs. As Catholic historian Christopher Dawson observed

> [T]he immense extension of the scale of education and its ramifications into a hundred specialisms and technical disciplines has left the [secular] state as the only unifying element in the whole system. In the past the traditional system of classical education provided a common intellectual background and a common scale of values with transcended and

> national and political frontiers and formed the European or Western republic of letters of which every scholar was a citizen.

While Christians may treat history in a philosophical manner, strictly speaking, there is no such thing as a "philosophy of history." This point may seem recondite, yet it is at the heart of modern misapprehension. History is an order or a process in time. This process, as St. Augustine explained, is not in itself an essence or a substance. It is the post-Christian thinkers like Voltaire, Hegel and Marx who erred on this point, trying to create a "philosophy of history" by which human events could be treated as predictable "patterns" and materially quantifiable "forces."

From a Christian perspective the outcome is assumed, but there is little specificity as to how this will come about. History is the work of Divine Providence, which realizes in time the eternal plan of God. This implies not only the Creation but also the Redemption of the human race in the fullness of time. Genuine historical study must, therefore, be Christocentric, based on an Incarnational perspective.

> Full completion comes... when [Jesus] places his kingship in the hands of God, his Father, having first dispossessed every other sort of rule, authority, and power; his reign, as we know, must continue until he has put all his enemies under his feet, and the last of those enemies to be dispossessed is death (I Cor. 15:24-25).

The Incarnation, the birth of Christ, by its very nature occurring in time, nevertheless points out another dimension, originating from eternity and pointing to eternity. "To the Christian," says Frederick Coppleston, S.J., "history is necessarily of profound importance. It was in history that man fell, in history that he was redeemed: it is in history, progressively, that the Body of Christ on earth grows and develops and that God's plan is unfolded." More specifically it was St. Augustine who "saw in history, as he saw in the individual, the struggle between two principles of conduct, two loves," the love of God on the one hand and the love of self on the other.

All events must be seen in this light. Not that we share God's omniscience but that we know that it is in operation. This outlook was taken for granted until the late Middle Ages, but with the rise of a skeptical form of humanism in the Renaissance, history began to be fragmented into artificial periods in order to accommodate it to personal and philosophical bias. The Incarnational view—never precisely formulated because it was simply taken for granted in an age of vibrant faith—survived less and less with the physical decline of Christendom. To better understand the post-Renaissance historiographical predicament, it may be helpful to review the birth and growth of historical studies in Western culture.

Following the long prehistoric period of mankind there emerged early civilizations whose original written records provide the first firms of historical documentation. At this point we enter the factual study of the past. Most nations and races have had folk memories to start with but only three have developed (independently) the concept of formal written history: a) the Chinese, b) the Hebrews, and c) the Greeks. The poet Homer was rooted in the epic genre recounting great events and people with the necessary mythic trappings. The purpose of this early bardic tradition was educational. The narrative was handed down from generation to generation and provided the models for the formation of the citizen of the ancient city-state.

The disciplined description of the past originates with Herodotus who is considered the "Father of History." Thucydides developed the idea further in *The Peloponnesian War*—which detailed the bloody civil war between Athens and Sparta—under which form it essentially passed to the Romans. By the time that Polybius was writing his chronicles of Rome, he confidently spoke of history as a "profitable field of knowledge." He also said it was strange that anyone, "however commonplace or indifferent, cannot be curious to learn how the whole world fell under undisputed ascendancy of Rome within the period of less than fifty-three years." One notes the change in genre. Unlike the Homeric epic, Polybius tried to provide an exact chronology.

This profitable field of knowledge, a systematic study of the past, became an intellectual discipline, invented by the Greeks and Romans in an approximate time span of four centuries. It was already called *historia*, a separate field of study (though it was never a separate *ars* of the seven liberal arts; it was studied as part of two comprehensive *artes*, grammar and rhetoric). Polybius expresses well its concept of self-contained meaning, though his understanding is quite removed from the later, false "philosophy of history" coined by the rationalists. Rather, Polybius' meaning was in the underlying goal that history revealed for mankind. He was referring to the empires, those great political, cultural and linguistic entities, proceeding in succession through the centuries: Babylon, Persia, and Alexander's conquests giving way to the Roman Empire.

St. Augustine echoes this by saying that "we must ascribe to the true God alone the power to grant kingdoms and empires" and that God "granted dominion to the Romans" just as He "gave sovereignty to the Assyrians, and also to the Persians." It is not accidental that the Incarnation and the subsequent establishment of the Church took place at a specific time and place—within the frontiers of the Roman world. This new development saw the convergence of three elements, each seemingly separate in origin, yet all tending towards a definite culmination. Hebrew religion, Greek philosophy and Roman order formed the triune structure of Christian Europe, perfectly personified by St. Paul, a Hellenized Jew and citizen of Rome.

According to the classical liberal view of the "Enlightenment," as brilliantly but erroneously expounded by Edward Gibbon in *The Decline and Fall of the Roman Empire*, Rome was "the period in the history of the world, during which the condition of the human race was most happy and prosperous." Gibbon's thesis that barbarian invasions and the rise of Christianity caused the downfall of the Western Empire became a stock-in-trade argument. It has hardly diminished in the two hundred years since he wrote his book.

Unlike other secularizers, Gibbon's "philosophy of history" is anti-historicist in that he sees no plan or progression in human events. He believed that the succession of events have no meaning and it is up to the historian to give it one. In this sense he is more honest than liberals who claim to see inevitable social forces at work. Still, Gibbon was imposing his own view on the past, and it is one which does not bear up to impartial study. The moral deterioration of the ancient empire set in well before the triumph of Christianity, and it was the Church, particularly the monastic institutions, which actually preserved what could still be preserved of Rome. Had it not been for this, Europe would have lapsed into a true Dark Age from which it would never have recovered. But there is little point in speculating about alternate versions of the past since its unfolding is neither random nor aimless.

The ancient Roman historians believed in the empire's eternity, as voiced by Virgil, "*Imperium sine fine dedi*" ("Empire without end have I granted," Jupiter declares in the *Aeneid*). St. Augustine presented the ultimate teleological understanding of the past with clear reference to providence which justified the idea of Rome in a way that even Virgil, the great eulogist of the Empire, had failed to do. The concept of a highly developed political and social order, the imperium, both preceded the Rome of the Caesars and survived it.

The Near East was the cradle of civilization, though we seldom appreciate what that means. Students briefly memorize the publication of Hammurabi's legal code in 1750 B.C. and then happily forget about the clay tablets and Ziggurats of Babylon. Yet Hammurabi's legal system—highly developed and enlightened for its time—was the prototype for subsequent legal codices of the Western world. The forms may have changed over time, nevertheless the core idea of a unified system of law endured and reached its culmination in early Christian history with the Code of Justinian I in 535 A.D.

This underlying civilizational ideal of the empire, its sense of order and justice, persisted in the concept of *Romanitas* ("Roman-ness") in the Middle Ages. The devotion of both sacred and lay rulers to upholding the values of Latin culture reveals an intuitive understanding of a transcendent purpose behind human development as well as a linear movement towards a supreme end. It is opposed to the pagan cyclical concept of history (*historia repetitur*) which has, not surprisingly, resurfaced in the works of writers since the Enlightenment.

The Christian view does not glorify the Empire for its own sake in the way that many humanists and liberals have. St. Augustine was not an apologist for pagan Rome and the first half of the City of God is largely a catalog of the evils of those who denied the true faith. Nevertheless the Bishop of Hippo believed that once the natural strengths of the Empire were subordinated to revealed religion, they would benefit the latter and aid its growth. While ungodly rulers were patently unjust and exercised only a semblance of true authority, so Christian emperors would establish political justice thereby benefiting the faithful. No further proof is needed than Constantine's Edict of Milan (313 A.D.) which ensured freedom of worship for Christians and the subsequent rapid establishment of new dioceses throughout the Empire. It is the working out on a global scale of the Thomistic dictum that the supernatural is built on the natural.

To some, this close identification of Christian civilization with the Roman world invites a mistaken view of the past. After all, the history of Rome and early Europe is fraught with superficial contradictions and disappointments, with political and social decline, feudal warfare and economic collapse. What this tells us, however, is that a purely state-sponsored culture, typical in Oriental nations, would not have survived the disasters that beset the late Empire. Unlike Christianized Rome, such a society is not truly dynamic. In those places where the political and social order became absolutely identical, culture is rendered static as happened in Egypt and China (and perhaps once again in the increasingly socialized Western states).

The concept of *imperium* came to fruition under Christianity and thus defies categorization as a mere political construct. It emerged from the collapse of the Western Empire because it was not strictly identical with the Rome of the Caesars. While coextensive with the Church's spiritual life, there being a clear and necessary interaction between the two, it was not identical with it either. The spiritual will always take priority over the material. Paradoxically this supernatural dimension is the key to the survivability of the Roman ideal, in that it was taken up and nurtured by a force greater than itself, whereas anything less would have engendered decay.

Things like social discipline, artistic expression, military power or economic competition do not exist for their own sakes, and when treated as self-sufficient ends they become perverted and even destructive. This is especially true for an advanced culture. The Incarnational view does not admit of any simplistic solution to societal problems and understands that this tension between the secular and the sacred is never fully resolved on this plane. It imposes a necessary striving for balance and is the source of vibrancy in our culture which sets it apart from all others, not only Eastern nations, but also the old pagan world. For Christians, perhaps the best proof of the providential nature of the development of the Roman concept lies in its robust continuity despite the shifting political topography of Europe.

Firstly, God does not measure success and failure in the way that we do. With the benefit of hindsight we can often see triumph amid failure. Likewise disaster will loom up amid apparent victory. The concept of *imperium* shifted from Rome to Constantinople and then was miraculously taken up by the very people who had nearly destroyed it — the Franks and the Germans. The collapse of Byzantium did not spell the end of our civilization. The Eastern Empire had departed from Rome both religiously and culturally. Its ecclesiastics evolved into a political appendage of the state (a situation which later prevailed in Orthodox Russia). Lacking the necessary moral independence of their Catholic counterparts, Byzantium's life resembled more and more the inert societies of the Orient. Outwardly superior in political and military strength, Constantinople would be eclipsed by the true renascence of Rome under the converted barbarians of the West.

Secondly, the fact that the Christian commonwealth has never been restricted to one nation or people again demonstrates God's intervention for the purpose of evangelization and also continually reinvigorating, as it were, the human side of the Church. Hence at many points in history the civilizing mission was exercised by multiple states simultaneously. French, German, Spanish and Slavic peoples variously took the lead in the Catholic social order, with the smaller nations also finding a meaningful and valuable role within a scheme that fostered complimentarity rather than crass competitiveness or bland conformity.

The Germans embraced the imperial concept in the form of the multiethnic Holy Roman Empire, later transformed into the Habsburg Empire of Austria-Hungary which provided 1,000 years of stability in Central Europe. Spain was the bulwark against militant Islam and led the way in a phenomenal conquest and conversion of the New World. France became the nexus of Europe both geographically and intellectually. It was a much needed point of stability for the outer marches of Christendom; a citadel to those embattled realms which formed our frontier against the savage and infidel. Even England, though not a "superpower" prior to the Reformation, left its enduring imprint on the West thanks to such intellects as the Venerable Bede, John of Salisbury and St. Thomas More. Nor does this unity in diversity (as understood in the original Christian sense) end with the recent cultural and religious decline of Europe. Evangelization continues and the role of Catholic peoples, in the Americas and Asia, is a story still unfolding.

As Malcolm Muggeridge wrote: "Thus can be seen, underlying the chaos of the world and of a spectator's own mind, God's order." The fact that the Christian nations have sadly been at odds with one another does not disprove the truth of Western unity, but reminds us of the fallen nature of mankind and the inability to put our confidence in a purely political settlement. Unlike other non-Christian societies, the rise and decline of individual states never threatened our cultural survival, and to some extent the inability of any single state to dominate Christendom acted as a safeguard against the absolutism which confronted the Church throughout its history (as for example, under Emperor Frederick II or Louis XIV). Standing at the opposite extreme from barbarian anarchy is total state control. Both are deviations from the mean of classical polity. Only in recent centuries, when the influence of the Church has been eliminated or reduced, has this absolutism advanced to a degree unthinkable to ancient tyrants in the form of crushing totalitarianism. By contrast, older Christian Europe survived and even flourished in the midst of political upheaval, invasions by barbarians and infidels, and devastating plagues, proving that it is not external but internal enemies that really threaten the *imperium* of Christian culture. It is loss of morale in the form of a spiritual collapse that corrodes society.

If the timeless concept of civilization has virtually disappeared, it is not because it is no longer viable. There is no greater need for an "Incarnational" ordering of society than today. But, as with the early Church surrounded by hostile pagan powers, the vision of *Romanitas* may pass into eclipse only to be brought back, perhaps even more resilient and vital than before, by the restoration of true Christian life.

Existentially Christian

Existentialism is understood as a modern philosophical movement—begun in the 19th century and culminating in the 20th—which stresses the uniqueness of individual experience in a hostile or indifferent universe. It sees our existence as inexplicable, and stresses freedom of choice and responsibility for the consequences of personal actions. In its most extreme form, this viewpoint is anti-teleological, nonconformist and atheistic. Such are the views of writers like Heidegger, Sartre and Camus. But when the Christian speaks of existentialism, he does so not as a self-sufficient creed (which is perhaps the great unintended irony of modern existentialism) but as a *method* or *approach*. As such, it offers interesting challenges and perspectives. Speaking of St. Thomas Aquinas, Jacques Maritain explains that his "existentialism"

> is utterly different from that of the "existentialist" philosophies propounded nowadays. If I say that it is, in my opinion, the only authentic existentialism, the reason is not that I am concerned to "rejuvenate" Thomism… by attempting to trick out Thomas Aquinas in a costume fashionable to our day…. A Thomist who speaks of St. Thomas's existentialism is merely reclaiming his own… he is asserting a prior right. [1]

[1] Jaques Maritain. *Existence and the Existent.* New York: Pantheon Books, 1948.

In this sense, existentialism should mean pure, unadulterated realism. At least, that is the chief boast of its modern proponents. Unfortunately, for many devotees, the alleged attempt to cut through the layers of rationalistic abstraction, which has blanketed man from reality and responsibility, has merely resulted in the proliferation of vast, obscurantist and often impenetrable systemization. Apropos of this is Søren Kierkegaard's parable:

> In relation to their systems most systematizers are like a man who builds an enormous castle and lives in a shack close by; they do not live in their own enormous systematic buildings. But spiritually that is a decisive objection. Spiritually speaking a man's thought must be the building in which he lives—otherwise everything is topsy-turvy.

Beginning with Kierkegaard, existentialists made a sharp distinction between "objectivity" and "subjectivity," opting for the latter as an antidote to dehumanizing materialist views that were increasingly popular. This dichotomy is understandable, but regrettable. It is due to an unnecessary confusion between "objectivity" and so-called "rationalism." During the 18th and 19th centuries, rationalists improperly associated empirical truth with their own limited powers of observation.

Intellection and abstraction, whereby we contemplate essences drawn from the data of our sense experience, are necessary to philosophy. In that sense "objectivatization" is not a dehumanizing betrayal of man's purpose. It is a necessary mental function and one that complements our "subjective" activities. All action, including moral decisions, requires man's will. Reason by itself presents the means and ends, but without will, nothing can be achieved. Yet without reason, our will becomes arbitrary and self-defeating.

St. Thomas, enlisting the help of Aristotle, defends the existent against the recurring tendency to take idealism to extremes—the belief that the physical world is somehow a deceptive "shadow land" compared to the world of the forms, as conceived by the mind. St. Thomas continually emphasizes the realm of sense knowledge. Further, only individual subjects exercise the act of existing. Hence the practice of religion, says Maritain, deals not with abstract "objects," but allows man to enter into a relationship of "subject to subject." Faith is "essentially that which no philosophy can be: a relation of person to person with all the risk, the mystery, the dread, the confidence, the delight, and the torment that lies in such a relationship."

Unfortunately, many thinkers responded to empiricism by seeking refuge in an "anti-rationalist" view. This is true of the romanticists as well as early existentialists like Kierkegaard and Dostoyevksy. Such a philosophy is considered immediate and tangible, hence personally verifiable, in a way that purely theoretical systems are not. Kierkegaard considered that his own strongly held Christian beliefs were validated by this approach.

Certainly no one attains religious belief by logical analysis alone. What is needed is a "leap of faith." The Danish thinker therefore goes beyond philosophy to account for incongruous qualities of man's flawed nature, such as base inclinations battling with nobler aspirations. He opposes the "objective analysis" or pure idealism of Kant. It is not possible to simply "think" our way through life's choices. We must live them. The answer is the passion of faith and surrender to God.

As Roger Shinn states in *The Existentialist Posture*: "Every belief tells us something about the believer. A man's personal commitments are part of the truth or falsity he declares."[2] It is a wonderful elucidation. It is also an apt retort to that craven utilitarianism which holds that the idealist should never be held accountable for his actions. Unfortunately, if it is true (as existentialists assert) that the key to a man's beliefs are his actions, then some of the foremost advocates of atheist existentialism are open to scrutiny. When their actions belie their claims to "authenticity," they are shown up to be fundamentally anti-existentialist—i.e., anti-reality. Jean Paul Sartre is perhaps the most egregious example.[3]

Kierkegaard was a dissenter from the new totalitarianism of "reason." His protest was against the new gnosticism of the philosophers.[4] He articulated the view of the ancient Christian mystics for whom God was grasped intuitively, by a love that is beyond mere reason, since *caritas* is greater than even the greatest human knowledge. Such a view is redolent of the "cloud of unknowing" or the *via negationis*, the doctrine of divine simplicity, of St. Thomas—according to this "eliminative method," one can define God by what he is not, since it is so difficult for us to truly appreciate what He is.[5]

---

[2] *The Existentialist Posture* (1970) is a readable and concise treatment, albeit from a liberal Christian perspective. Another helpful study for the layman (currently in print) is *Dostoevsky, Kierkegaard, Nietzsche and Kafka* by William Hubben.

[3] For more details, see Brian C. Anderson's essay "The Absolute Intellectual" (*Policy Review*, February 2004) and Thomas Molnar's full-length study, *Sartre: Ideologue of Our Time* (1968). Sartre's career in the French Resistance was of his own invention. After 1945, Sartre compounded fraud with opportunism by riding on the coattails of post-war Communist vogue, penning embarrassing apologias for Stalin's mass murders. This was too much even for his fellow existentialist, Albert Camus.

[4] Needless to say, Kierkegaard's own views were problematic. He was a critic rather than a formulator of a positive system, and self-consciously at odds with institutional worship, though he offered striking insights into certain philosophical difficulties.

[5] St. Thomas does not say that we can make no true assertions about the first existent, but only that we cannot have any comprehensive knowledge of him on the scientific model.

Of course, there are incipient problems in any existentialist philosophy. Man is supposedly faced with a dissonance between "essence" and "existence." Sartre even held that "existence precedes essence." But as Maritain argues, existence is impossible without essence. It is essence (or nature) that provides us with universals, something that not even Sartre can reject without contradicting himself, for example, in trying to establish what is good or "authentic" for all human beings.

Classical philosophy tells us that truth is conformity of the mind with a reality that it does not make. The idealist philosophers, however, saw nature as a raw material out of which the mind can build entirely new structures of reality. Later existentialists, like Friedrich Nietzche, accepted and modified this belief and posited the primacy of the will over the mind in redefining man's environment. There is an appropriate irony in the way that rationalist exaggeration of human intellect, having rebelled against normative truth, found itself demoted in turn. Unfortunately, it sends us farther along the path of error.

A more basic difficulty in existentialism lies in making "feeling" the basis for truth. This is the case even for theistic existentialists. Rationality is not the enemy, though its misuse makes it seem oppressive. For the Christian there is a paradox in that reason must be humiliated, but only in order to preserve it in its proper sphere. It is the necessary basis of liberty since it permits us to exercise prudence and to reflect upon our moral choices. Realist philosophy sides with the early existentialists in their defense of free will against fatalistic idealism. Unfortunately, the final development of existentialism has been to reject reason completely in favor of a "pure liberty" which becomes nihilism in more sense than one. Kierkegaard foresaw the rift that would divide later existentialists. There were those, like Heidegger, for whom mere "willing" was enough. The Danish existentialist knew that one must specifically *will the good.* There is a difference between "content" and mere "passion" of belief.

Of all the issues looming in the existentialist universe that which garners the most attention is the crisis of "alienation." Kierkegaard grappled with the question, postulating that man was cast adrift by a fashionable agnosticism and the apparent lack of metaphysical authority. The result was emptiness and uncertainty. In this way, existentialism (as an *ism*) could almost be described as byproduct of modern *angst.* Yet we can find hints of this identity crisis even earlier, in St. Augustine and Boethius.

While other developments in existentialism may be of doubtful value, it is the *ethical* predicament—the scope of man's free will and its consequences—that seizes our attention. "All morality," says Maritain, "hangs upon that which is most existential in the world. For love… does not deal with possibles or pure essences, it deals with existents." Likewise in the exercise of prudence, while relying on universals for guidance, every decision brings into existence a unique act. No knowledge of essences, however detailed, can exempt one from the judgment of conscience. At the same time, as Maritain notes, a philosophy of pure action (*praxis*) and pure liberty—maintained in the academic existentialism of the 20th century—must result in a denial of existence. Jean-Paul Sartre clearly blundered in this direction with his famous treatise *Being and Nothingness.*

In Book IV of the *Consolation of Philosophy* (*c.* 524 A.D.), Boethius asks us to reflect "on the crippling paralysis which grips the wicked…. They fail in their quest for the supreme crown of reality, for the wretched creatures do not succeed in attaining that outcome" for which they struggle. Boethius adopts even more startling language, presaging later thinkers. He argues that wicked men "do not exist in an absolute sense." Evil men possess a kind of power, but it stems not from their strength but their weakness, "for they can perform evil things, whereas had they been able to continue doing good things, they could certainly not have performed evil ones. The capability which they do have shows more clearly that they have no power." This is because "evil is nothing." Or as St. Thomas puts it, "All that comes from nothing tends of itself towards nothing."

John Navone has noted the causes and effects of ego-centered behavior and the frustration it engenders. For example, an exaggerated self-assessment can cause one to be out of touch with oneself. We can be also be "guilty of living in and for the future [living only for our own plans], neglecting the importance of the present moment. In doing so, we become rather remote.... Our inattention to what we may reasonably anticipate alienates us from who we are."[6]

Because rationalists abandoned belief in a personal God, thus "obviating" personal responsibility, subsequent generations reacted against this by insisting on "experience" alone. To quote Kierkegaard again:

> Fundamentally Hegel makes men into heathens, *into a race of animal gifted with reason.* For in the animal world "the individual" is always less important than the race. But it is the peculiarity of the human race that just because the individual is created in the image of God "the individual" is above the race.

There is much truth in this. Yet in neither natural nor supernatural life are we thrown back entirely on our own devices. We are formed to some degree communally and hi-

---

[6] Rev. John Navone. "The Nearness of God." *Homiletic & Pastoral Review.* June 2005.

erarchically, be it within the family, school, the state, or the Church. Such relationships are organic and complementary to the individual's needs. As Stanley L. Jaki says of the conversion of Newman, the Church is "the concretely existential means set up by Christ to implement salvation for any and all."[7] But the jettisoning of authority (so lamented by Kierkegaard) has permitted the impulses towards collectivism and individualism to spin off in their own mutually destructive directions.

We must acknowledge the difficulty that has dogged even the best existentialist efforts. The movement is largely a rhetorical and literary one. Existentialism successfully postulates questions in ways that resonate with our own intimate experience; yet this very strength it also its greatest weakness. Such an outlook easily leads to solipsism, or the view that limits reality to one's personal situations. Hence Maritain concludes that a "Christian Existentialism" (as a theo-philosophy) is neither necessary nor possible. Yet a Christian *understanding of the existential* resolves itself into a simple fact. To deny God's existence is to be out of touch with God, and oneself. Indeed, that is the point of departure between a theistic and atheistic definition of the existent. For the former, Thomas à Kempis' observation in the *Imitation of Christ* is true. "Before God I am empty nothingness, a weak and unstable man.... Can nothing boast of its nothingness?" The nothingness is within, yet capable of being healed by the infinite love of its Creator. Hence, the Christian virtue of humility is not based on sentimentality but on an acknowledgement of reality. The believer recognizes the marvelous and unmerited fact of his existence as bestowed by the First Existent (God).

---

[7] Stanley L. Jaki. "Newman: Myth and Facts." *New Oxford Review*. November 2001.

By contrast, in the Sartrean universe, the ego is the only reality surrounded by nothingness. The self is relentlessly oppressed by objects (obstacles or limits) which frustrate its desires, resulting in alienation. In defiance, the individual asserts meaning through acts, regardless of the quality of those acts, since any universal reference point of good and evil has been eliminated. Indeed, the *only* "evil" lies in constraints placed on man's activity. This permits Sartre to (quite literally) venerate Jean Genet, a convict and sexual pervert who became the poster child of the leftist intelligentsia after World War II.[8]

Such is the exaggeration of existentialist isolationism to the point that man is impelled headlong by blind impulses. The result is an escape from personal responsibility which takes refuge in determinism. Life is a chain of meaningless events according to the law of cause and effect. As a result, man's remaining aspiration is to justify his existence by bearing the burden of a pointless universe. But the mind (like nature) abhors a vacuum. Such fatalism led Sartre to embrace Marxism. It was the apparent negation of his earlier radical individualism, yet the two creeds ultimately meet in their denial of the transcendent.

Recalling us to Christian realism, Thomas à Kempis says, "Empty conceit is like an evil disease, and the most monstrous of vanities, for it leads man away from true glory." By indulging in these "monstrous vanities," we are left to wallow in an emptiness of our own selfish creation. It is what theologians would describe as our ability to resist grace and thus cut ourselves off from God, the true reality and basis of existence. On the other hand, as Maritain concludes, the au-

[8] This inspired Sartre's celebration of moral nihilism in *Saint Genet* (1952).

thentic exercise of free will necessitates charity since it presumes the "generosity of existence" created by Another.

Acknowledgements

I am grateful to Sidonius Lepsi, O.C.S.C. (1934-2000), my intellectual and spiritual mentor for many years, for his notes which formed the basis of "God and History" and "The Anthropology of Monotheism." Prof. Lepsi was an émigré from the former Communist state of Czechoslovakia, and spent his final years as a college instructor in the United States. Working in the tradition of Christopher Dawson, he applied himself to all levels of historical study, humbly imparting his encyclopedic knowledge to others with the aim of furthering not only their understanding of the liberal arts but also their Catholic faith.

Michael Hennessy, English lecturer and researcher on the Catholic literary revival, edited the essay on Hilaire Belloc's *The Four Men.*

Finally, this collection would not have been possible without the kind permission of Dr. Grahame Clough (*The Bellocian*), Fr. Kenneth Baker (*Homiletic & Pastoral Review*), John Blewett (*Latin Mass Magazine*) and Peter Miller (*Seattle Catholic*) to reprint essays from their respective journals. Revisions have been made to many of the texts as originally published.

The Bellocian: "All Saints and the Sussex Countryside"(Vol. 7, No. 1 [2004]); *Homiletic & Pastoral Review*: "Philosophy and the Early Church" (December 2004). *Latin Mass Magazine*: "Yesterday's Tomorrow" (orig. "Paradise Lost: The Quest for the Perfect Future," Spring 2004); "Inventing Hitler" (Summer 2003), "Rousseau's Daycare" (Winter 2005); "An Approach to Apologetics" (orig. "Book Review: The Catholic Church and History," Winter 2003); "The Man Behind the Mask" (orig. "Book Review: The Unmasking of Oscar Wilde," Fall 2004). *Seattle Catholic*: "God and History" (August 30, 2004); "Christianity and the Pursuit of Leisure" (December 28, 2005); "The Anthropology of Monotheism" (orig. "From Many Gods to One?," October 13, 2004); "The Psychology of Unbelief" (October 12, 2005).

Printed in the United Kingdom
by Lightning Source UK Ltd.
131376UK00002B/362/P

9 780615 199122